Trend H

Trend Horses

Form Breakers for the Jumps 2009-2010

Andrew Mount

With thanks to…

Julian Brown and his team at Raceform

Bill and Janet for the proof reading

All the Trend Horses readers who contacted me after Mon Mome's 100-1 Grand National win. In reply to the question 'Did you back him?' the answer is 'Yes, I had plenty on … unfortunately for the Welsh National three months earlier.'

Cover photograph: Punjabi (Barry Geraghty, right) wins the Champion Hurdle as the 2009 Cheltenham Festival from Binocular (Tony McCoy). Copyright © Edward Whitaker/Racing Post

Published in 2009 by Raceform Ltd
High Street, Compton, Newbury, Berkshire RG20 6NL

A catalogue record for this book is available from the British Library.

ISBN 978-1-906820-19-0

Designed by Fiona Pike

Printed in the UK by CPI William Clowes Beccles NR34 7TL

Contents

About the Author

ANDREW MOUNT is a journalist and leading racing advisor. He has written (or co-written) several best-selling books about horseracing including...

SprintLine 2002: incorporating the effects of the draw
(with Graham Wheldon and David Renham)
Trend Horses: Form Breakers for the Jumps and All-Weather Flat
(with Peter Stavers)
Form-Breakers for the Flat
Trend Horses: Form Breakers for the Jumps
Trend Horses: Drawn2win (with David Renham)
Trend Horses for the Jumps 2005 & All-weather Flat 2004/05
Trend Horses for the Flat & Summer Jumps 2005
Trend Horses: Form Breakers for the Jumps 2005/06
Trend Horses: Form Breakers for the Flat 2006
Trend Horses: Form Breakers for the Jumps 2006/07
Trend Horses: Form Breakers for the Flat 2007
Trend Horses: Form Breakers for the Jumps 2007/08
Trend Horses: Form Breakers for the Flat 2008
Trend Horses: Form Breakers for the Jumps 2008/09
Trend Horses: Form Breakers for the Flat 2009

His Trend Horses column can be found on the **GG.com** website and he also writes for *Raceform Update*.

Introduction

What Are Trend Horses?

Trend Horses are racehorses that have shown a strong preference for a certain set of race conditions. My aim is to uncover these patterns in order to identify potentially profitable bets. .

Noticeable preferences may include one or more of the following; the need for a particular distance or going, for a small or large field, for a very recent outing or a long absence between races, for a certain class of race, for a flat or undulating course, or for a right-handed or left-handed track.

Here is a simple example:

TRICKY TRICKSTER (IRE)
6yo b g (P F Nicholls)

He's a six-year-old bay gelding trained by Paul Nicholls. To begin with, I break down his career form figures by race type …

Race type	Ptp: 1 (1-1)
	Hdl: 42 (0-2)
	Chs: 2121 (2-4)
Conclusion:	he's best over fences.

Then by race distance …

Distance	2m4f-2m7.5f: 4222 (0-4)
	3m-3m2.5f+: 11 (2-2)
	4m+: 1 (1-1)
Conclusion:	he needs at least 3m and stays marathon trips.

Then by going …

Going	Good or faster: no runs
	Good to yielding: 1 (1-1)
	Good to soft: 421 (1-3)
	Soft: 21 (1-2)
	Heavy: 2 (0-1)
Conclusion:	he is suited by plenty of cut in the ground

Using the information uncovered above I reach the following conclusion …
Summary of ideal conditions Combine chase starts with racing over 3m or further and his record becomes: 111 (3-3).

This book contains over 150 similar examples but if I could pick just 10 to follow this coming Jumps season I'd opt for these:

BESHABAR (IRE)
DEFINITY (IRE)
LE BURF (FR)
MALJIMAR (IRE)
PAGAN STARPRINCESS
PREISTS LEAP (IRE)
RING BO REE (IRE)
SPANISH CRUISE (IRE)
THEATRICAL MOMENT (USA)
WISE MEN SAY (IRE)

As per usual, I'll be contributing to the Angle Finders column in *Raceform Update* (out every Wednesday), producing a free-to-read Trend Horses column for the GG.com website and giving daily selections on my Trend Horses Pro subscription service (details on the GG.com website).

Best of luck

Andrew Mount

Course Descriptions

Course	Description
Aintree	Two left-handed courses. Grand National circuit, 2m2f, is flat and has big fences with drop on landing side and a long run-in. Mildmay Course, 1m3f, flat with conventional fences, is sharper than the hurdles course. 11.98% of chase runners fell or unseated on the Mildmay Course last season. 29.84% of chase runners fell or unseated on the Grand National Course, well down on the previous season's figures.
Ascot	Right-handed, galloping, last mile mainly uphill, with stiff fences. Circuit 1m5f. Approximately 10.15% of runners fell or unseated their riders on the chase course last season (five-year figure = 8.62%).
Ayr	Left-handed, mainly flat. Circuit 1m4f. 13.43% of chase runners fell or unseated last term (five-year figure = 10.48%).
Bangor	Left-handed, sharp and flat with a long run-in. Circuit 1m4f. 3.74% fell or unseated last term (five-year figure = 6.17%).
Carlisle	Right-handed, undulating, stiff and galloping. Circuit 1m5f. 5.41% of chase runners fell or unseated last season (five-year figure = 4.17%).
Cartmel	Left-handed, sharp and undulating, with a four-furlong run-in for chases. Circuit 1m. 10.29% of chase runners fell or unseated during the 2008/2009 season, as compared to a five-year average of 6.88%.
Catterick	Left-handed, sharp and undulating, suiting handy types. Circuit 1m3f. 10.29% of chase runners fell or unseated last season (five-year average = 11.23%).
Cheltenham (old)	Left-handed, galloping, undulating and testing track with stiff fences. Circuit 1m4f.
Cheltenham (new)	Left-handed, galloping, undulating and testing track with stiff fences. Circuit 1m4½f. 9.78% fell or unseated on the above two courses combined last term, as compared to a five-year average of 10.67% (figures do not include cross-country races).

Chepstow   Left-handed and undulating. Going can be very testing. Circuit 1m7f. 8.63% of chase runners fell or unseated last season (five-year average = 7.87%).

Doncaster   Left-handed, galloping, generally flat. Heavy ground rare. Circuit 2m. 6.28% of chase runners fell or unseated last season (five-year average = 8.83%).

Exeter   Right-handed and undulating. Stiff test of stamina. Circuit 2m. Only 2.61% of chase runners fell or unseated last season (five-year average = 8.28%).

Fakenham   Left-handed, sharp, undulating. Circuit 1m. 12.44% of chase runners fell or unseated last season (five-year average = 10.89%).

Ffos Las   Left-handed, flat, galloping.

Folkestone   Right-handed undulating oval of 1m2f. 7.17% of chase runners fell or unseated last season (five-year average = 4.81%).

Fontwell   Left-handed hurdle course and figure-of-eight chase course. Ground can be testing. Circuit 1m. 9.46% of chase runners fell or unseated last season (five-year average = 8.27%).

Haydock   Left-handed, flat and galloping. Chase course now on hurdles track and with portable fences. New course sharper than the old track. Circuit 1m4f. 5.61% of chase runners fell or unseated last season (five-year average = 5.84%).

Hereford   Right-handed, sharpish and generally flat. Circuit 1m4f. 7.65% of chase runners fell or unseated last season (five-year average = 7.73%).

Hexham   Left-handed, severe and undulating, placing emphasis on stamina. Circuit 1m4f. 5.47% of chase runners fell or unseated last season (five-year average = 7.44%).

Huntingdon   Right-handed, flat and galloping. Circuit 1m4f. 8.74% of chase runners fell or unseated last season (five-year average = 9.05%).

Kelso
Left-handed and undulating. Hurdles course of 1m1f is sharp, more so than 1m3f chase track, which has 2f run-in. 15.24% of chase runners fell or unseated last season (five-year average = 12.19%).

Kempton
Right-handed triangular circuit of 1m5f, practically flat. 9.06% of chase runners fell or unseated last season (five-year average = 7.96%).

Leicester
Right-handed and undulating, placing emphasis on stamina. Circuit 1m6f. 10.26% of chase runners fell or unseated last season (five-year average = 11.69%).

Lingfield
Left-handed, undulating and sharp. Chase circuit 1m5f, hurdles run on flatter course. 7.32% of chase runners fell or unseated last season (five-year average = 7.13%).

Ludlow
Right-handed. Chase course flat with sharp bends, circuit 1m4f. Hurdles track 150y longer, slightly undulating with easier bends. 6.01% of chase runners fell or unseated last season (five-year average = 7.46%).

Market Rasen
Right-handed oval, slightly undulating. Circuit 1m2f. 7.44% of chase runners fell or unseated last season (five-year average = 7.77%).

Musselburgh
Right-handed, virtually flat track with sharp turns. Circuit 1m3f. 13.50% of chase runners fell or unseated last season (five-year average = 11.58%).

Newbury
Left-handed, flat and galloping. Circuit 1m7f. 8.90% of chase runners fell or unseated last season (five-year average = 7.14%).

Newcastle
Left-handed, with uphill finish. Going can be very testing. Circuit 1m6f. 11.68% of chase runners fell or unseated last season (five-year average = 10.15%).

Newton Abbot
Left-handed oval, sharp with short run-in. Circuit 1m2f. 4.56% of chase runners fell or unseated last season (five-year average = 6.60%).

Perth
Right-handed and flat, with tight bends. Chase course has long run-in. Circuit 1m2f. 6.19% of chase runners fell or unseated last season (five-year average = 7.53%).

Plumpton
Left-handed, undulating, sharp. Circuit 1m1f. 13.08% of chase runners fell or unseated last season (five-year average = 12.40%).

Sandown
Right-handed with stiff uphill finish. Circuit 1m5f. 13.33% of chase runners fell or unseated last season (five-year average = 7.86%).

Sedgefield
Left-handed, undulating oval, sharp bends. Circuit 1m2f. 7.48% of chase runners fell or unseated last season (five-year average = 7.81%).

Southwell
Left-handed oval, approx 1m round, with six portable fences. Outside half of jumps course used in summer. 9.04% of chase runners fell or unseated last season (five-year average = 11.50%).

Stratford
Left-handed flat and sharp, with short finishing straight. Circuit 1m2f. 7.30% of chase runners fell or unseated last season (five-year average = 11.47%).

Taunton
Right-handed oval, on the sharp side with short run in. Circuit 1m2f. A massive 10.71% of chase runners fell or unseated last season (five-year average = 13.27%).

Towcester
Right-handed with last mile uphill. Very testing. Circuit 1m6f. 7.53% of chase runners fell or unseated last season (five-year average = 10.81%).

Uttoxeter
Left-handed with some undulations. Hurdle course is inside chase course. Circuit 1m3f. 4.52% of chase runners fell or unseated last season (five-year average = 6.83%).

Warwick
Left-handed with tight turns and short run-in. Circuit 1m5f. 5.63% of chase runners fell or unseated last season (five-year average = 9.89%).

Wetherby   Left-handed oval, with easy bends. Circuit 1m4f.13.62% of chase runners fell or unseated last season (five-year average = 11.02%).

Wincanton   Right-handed rectangular circuit. Mainly flat. Circuit 1m3f. 15.88% of chase runners fell or unseated last season (five-year average = 12.45%).

Worcester   Left-handed 1m5f oval, flat with long straights and easy turns. 5.96% of chase runners fell or unseated last season (five-year average = 6.25%).

A-Z OF TREND HORSES
(all horses' records correct as of 8 September 2009)

ACAMBO (GER)
8yo gr g (D Pipe)

Race type   Hdl: 1135011P660911 (6-14)
Chs: 1FP (1-3)

Conclusion: he won on his chase debut when 2-5 favourite in a four-runner race but has failed to complete the course in two subsequent outings over fences and seems far better over hurdles.

Distance   2m-2m1f: 1135011P16P911 (7-14)
2m3f-2m4f: 6F0 (0-3)

Conclusion: all his wins have come at trips of about 2m.

Going   Good to firm or faster: 1591 (2-4)
Good: 016F1 (2-5)
Good to soft: 1116P0 (3-6)
Soft: 3P (0-2)
Heavy: no runs

Conclusion: he seems best on good to soft or faster going.

Fresh   First two runs or when rested for five weeks+: 11011P61FP01 (6-12)
Others: 35691 (1-5)

Conclusion: he runs especially well when fresh.

Headgear   Visor: 0 (0-1)

Conclusion: he ran poorly when tried in a visor, finishing 23rd in the 2006 County Hurdle at the Cheltenham Festival.

Summary of ideal conditions Combine hurdle starts on good to soft or faster going with running over a distance of 2m-2m1f, when not wearing headgear, and his record becomes: 115116911 (6-9), improving to: 11111 (5-5) when fresh (first two starts each season or when rested for five weeks or longer thereafter).

AIMIGAYLE
6yo b m (Miss Suzy Smith)

Race type	
	NHF: 1 (1-1)
	Hdl: 0362371133140 (3-13)
	Chs: 2121U (2-5)
Conclusion:	she's effective over hurdles and fences.
Distance	2m-2m2.5f: 102 (1-3)
	2m3f-2m5.5f: 36371332240 (1-11)
	2m6f-2m7.5f: 11 (2-2)
	3m+: 11U (2-3)
Conclusion:	she has won all her completed starts over 2m6f or further.
Going	Good to firm or faster: 363 (0-3)
	Good: 1023711321110 (6-13)
	Good to soft: 24U (0-3)
	Soft/heavy: no runs
Conclusion:	she has avoided soft going throughout her career.
Field size	12 or more runners: 0314U0 (1-6)
	10-11 runners: no runs
	8-9 runners: 36271331211 (4-11)
	7 or fewer runners: 12 (1-2)
Conclusion:	she scraped home from 15 rivals in a weak handicap hurdle at Huntingdon in May 2008 but all her other wins have come in single-digit line-ups.
Track	Figure-of-8: 2 (0-1)
	Left-handed: 10271331U0 (3-10)
	Right-handed: 36311214 (3-8)
Conclusion:	she has jumped out to her right on occasions and might prove best when racing clockwise.

Summary of ideal conditions When racing over a distance of 2m6f or further her record reads: 1111U (4-5), improving to: 1111 (4-4) on good or faster going only.

AIR FORCE ONE (GER)
7yo ch g (C J Mann)

Race type	
	Hdl: 5112 (2-4)
	Chs: 611251122506P (4-13)
Conclusion:	he's effective over hurdles and fences.
Distance	2m4f-2m5f: 116 (2-3)
	2m6f+: 5211251122506P (4-14)
Conclusion:	he needs a trip of at least 2m4f.

Going	Good to firm or faster: no runs
	Good: 1211256 (3-7)
	Good to soft: 261520 (1-6)
	Soft/heavy: 511P (2-4)
Conclusion:	he has won a couple of weak races on soft going but seems happiest on good ground.
Track	Left-handed: 5265206 (0-7)
	Right-handed: 11121125P (5-9)
	Figure-of-eight: 1 (1-1)
Conclusion:	he has yet to win on a left-handed track.
Fresh	Seasonal debuts: 562 (0-3)
Conclusion:	he might need his first run of the season.
Field size	12 or more runners: 220P (0-4)
(chase runs	8-11 runners: 1556 (1-4)
only)	7 or fewer runners: 61211 (3-5)
Conclusion:	he has yet to win in a big field when racing over fences.

Summary of ideal conditions When racing over a distance of 2m4f or further, aside from seasonal debuts, his record is: 1121125112506P (6-14), improving to: 11112115P (6-9) if we discard his runs on left-handed tracks.

ALFRED'S TOWER
7yo b g (P F Nicholls)

Race type	Hdl: 469914 (1-6)
	Chs: 163F (1-4)
Conclusion:	he has winning form over hurdles and fences.
Distance	2m3f-2m6f: 4699161 (2-7)
	3m+: 3F4 (0-3)
Conclusion:	he has yet to win beyond 2m6f but was still in contention and travelling well before falling two from home over 3m1.5f at Wincanton in May 2009.
Going	Good to firm or faster: 14 (1-2)
	Good: 6F (0-2)
	Good to soft: 13 (1-2)
	Soft: 69 (0-2)
	Heavy: 49 (0-2)
Conclusion:	his best efforts have come on good to soft or softer going.
Track	Left-handed: 4694 (0-4)
	Right-handed: 91631F (2-6)
Conclusion:	both his wins came on right-handed tracks (Towcester and Wincanton).

Fresh (absence 42 days or longer: 41614 (2-5)
since last race) 41 days or less: 6993F (0-5)
Conclusion: both his wins came when running fresh in the spring (after breaks of 119 and 114 days).
Headgear Tongue-tie: 63 (0-2)
Conclusion: his two starts in a tongue-tie culminated in heavy defeats (by 36 and 34 lengths).
Summary of ideal conditions Combine hurdle or chase starts with running on good to soft or faster going and his record becomes: 1631F4 (2-6), improving to: 11F (2-3) when racing right-handed minus the tongue-tie.

AMERICAN TRILOGY (IRE)

5yo gr g (P F Nicholls)
Race type Hdl: 1249123 (2-7)
Conclusion: he is a useful hurdler and is likely to switch to fences in the autumn of 2009.
Distance 2m-2m1f: 134123 (2-6)
2m4f: 9 (0-1)
Conclusion: he didn't seem to stay 2m4f when tried over that trip at Ascot in February 2009.
Going Good to firm or faster: 3 (0-1)
Good: 2 (0-1)
Good to soft: 41 (1-2)
Soft: 13 (1-2)
Heavy: 9 (0-1)
Conclusion: he seems effective on any going.
Field size 16 or more runners: 11 (2-2)
12-15 runners: 49 (0-2)
11 or fewer runners: 323 (0-3)
Conclusion: both his hurdle wins came in huge line-ups (18 and 27 ran) and two of his three Flat wins in France also came in fields of 16+.
Summary of ideal conditions When racing at distances of about 2m his record is: 134123 (2-6), improving to: 11 (2-2) in fields of 16 or more runners. He's best coming late off a strong gallop and, if taking to fences, will be of particular interest for the 2010 Arkle Chase.

APOLLO CREED (IRE)

7yo b g (N A Twiston-Davies)

Race type	NHF: 4 (0-1)
	Hdl: 4541514 (2-7)
	Chs: 4F111622465 (3-11)
Conclusion:	he has a good strike-rate over hurdles and fences.
Distance	2m-2m2f: 441 (1-3)
	2m3f-2m7f: 54F5111225 (3-10)
	3m+: 441646 (1-6)
Conclusion:	the majority of his wins have come at trips short of 3m.
Going	Good to firm (good in places) or faster: 11162 (3-5)
	Good (good to firm in places): F16 (1-3)
	Good: 5146 (1-4)
	Good (good to soft in places): 4452 (0-4)
	Good to soft: no runs
	Soft/heavy: 444 (0-3)
Conclusion:	he is suited by fast going.
Time of year	Jan-Feb: 46 (0-2)
	Mar-Apr: F5 (0-2)
	May-Jun: 15141 (3-5)
	Jul-Aug: 1162 (2-4)
	Sep-Oct: 442 (0-3)
	Nov-Dec: 544 (0-3)
Conclusion:	all his wins have come in spring/summer.

Summary of ideal conditions When racing on good or faster going his record reads: 5F114111626 (5-11), improving to: F1141116 (5-8) if we only consider his runs from March to August.

ARALDUR (FR)

5yo ch g (A King)

Race type	Chs: 31114 (3-5)
Conclusion:	he won three of his five chase starts for Alan King last season.
Distance	2m-2m1f: 111 (3-3)
	2m1.5f+: 34 (0-2)
Conclusion:	his wins came at about 2m.
Going	Good to firm or faster: no runs
	Good: 3 (0-1)
	Good to soft: 114 (2-3)
	Soft: 1 (1-1)
	Heavy: no runs
Conclusion:	he seems ideally suited by good to soft or softer going.

Fresh (absence 42 days or longer: 34 (0-2)
since last race) 41 days or less: 111 (3-3)
Conclusion: all his wins came after a recent outing (25, 14 and 17 days).
Summary of ideal conditions When racing over fences his record reads: 31114 (3-5), improving to: 111 (3-3) if we only consider his runs at 2m, on good to soft or softer going and after a recent outing.

AT THE MONEY

6yo b g (J M P Eustace)

Race type	Hdl: 19672463150P631 (3-15)
Conclusion:	all his jumps runs have taken place over hurdles.
Distance	2m-2m2.5f: 124 (1-3)
	2m3f-2m5.5f: 9676363 (0-7)
	2m6f+: 150P1 (2-5)
Conclusion:	he won a weak 2m novice event at Warwick on his hurdles debut but his two subsequent wins have come over 2m6f (both at Market Rasen – a track that favours his running style).
Going	Good to firm or faster: no runs
	Good: 31 (1-2)
	Good to soft: 74306 (0-5)
	Soft: 9615P (1-5)
	Heavy: 126 (1-3)
Conclusion:	he's effective on good or softer going.
Field size	12 or more runners: 9246350P63 (0-10)
	11 or fewer runners: 16711 (3-5)
Conclusion:	he's a front-runner and is best able to dominate in small fields.

Summary of ideal conditions When racing over hurdles in fields of 11 or fewer runners his record reads: 16711 (3-5), with the two defeats excusable as he was ridden with more restraint than usual.

ATOUCHBETWEENACARA (IRE)

8yo b/br g (Tim Vaughan)

Race type	NHF: 2 (0-1)
	Hdl: 463 (0-3)
	Chs: 1F2F21 (2-6)
Conclusion:	both his wins – for previous trainer Venetia Williams – came over fences.
Distance	2m-2m2.5f: 23 (0-2)
	2m3f-2m5.5f: 61F21 (2-5)
	2m6f+: 4F2 (0-3)
Conclusion:	he pulled too hard when runner-up over 3m at Haydock last season and is likely to prove best at about 2m4f.
Going	Good to yielding or faster: 1F1 (2-3)
	Good to soft: 62F (0-3)
	Soft: 2432 (0-4)
	Heavy: no runs
Conclusion:	his best efforts have come on good going.
Fresh (absence since last race)	84 days or longer: 23121 (2-5)
	42-83 days: 6 (0-1)
	28-41 days: 2 (0-1)
	27 days or less: 4FF (0-3)
Conclusion:	he runs especially well when fresh.
Track	Left-handed: 63121 (2-5)
	Right-handed: 24F2F (0-5)
Conclusion:	he has yet to win on a right-handed track.

Summary of ideal conditions When racing over fences his record reads: F1F2F21 (2-7), improving to: 11 (2-2) if we only consider his left-handed runs at about 2m4f.

BALLY CONN (IRE)

7yo br g (M Hill)

Race type	NHF: 1 (1-1)
	Hdl: 56431133116 (4-11)
	Chs: PPP (0-3)
Conclusion:	he failed to complete in three starts over fences for former trainer Henrietta Knight.
Distance	2m: 1 (1-1)
	2m4f-2m5.5f: 61 (1-2)
	2m6f+: 54PPP3113316 (3-12)
Conclusion:	he has been campaigned over 2m4f or further since landing a Towcester bumper in November 2006.

Going	Good to firm or faster: no runs
	Good: 5PP3 (0-4)
	Good to soft: 4P311 (2-5)
	Soft: 3116 (2-4)
	Heavy: 16 (1-2)
Conclusion:	he needs good to soft or softer going.
Track	Left-handed: 4PP6 (0-4)
	Right-handed: 156P3113311 (5-11)
Conclusion:	he has yet to prove his effectiveness on left-handed tracks.
Trainer	Henrietta Knight: 1564PPP (1-7)
	Martin Hill: 31133116 (4-8)
Conclusion:	he has a 50% strike-rate for current trainer Martin Hill.

Summary of ideal conditions When running on good to soft or softer going for Martin Hill his record reads: 3113116 (4-7), improving to: 11311 (4-5) when racing right-handed after a recent outing.

BALLYFITZ

9yo b g (N A Twiston-Davies)

Race type	Hdl: 111271152 (5-9)
	Chs: U1122P (2-6)
Conclusion:	he won a couple of small-field chases last season but his jumping remains unconvincing.
Distance	2m4f-2m7f: 127 (1-3)
	3m+: 1U111521122P (6-12)
Conclusion:	he is best at 3m or further.
Going	Good or faster: 1U52 (1-4)
	Good to soft: 1112P (3-5)
	Soft: 12711 (3-5)
	Heavy: 2 (0-1)
Conclusion:	he seems to handle most conditions.
Class	1 (Grade 1, 2 or 3): 752P (0-4)
	1 (Listed): 1 (1-1)
	2: U12112 (3-6)
	3: 12 (1-2)
	4: 11 (2-2)
Conclusion:	all his wins have come in Listed or lower company.

Field size	12 or more runners: P (0-1)
(chase runs	8-11 runners: U (0-1)
only)	7 or fewer runners: 1122 (2-4)
Conclusion:	he has yet to complete the course when racing over fences in fields of more than seven runners.

Summary of ideal conditions When racing below Grade 3 level his record reads: 11U12112112 (7-11), improving to: 11112 (4-5) at 3m or further on good to soft or softer going.

BALLYGALLEY BOB (IRE)
8yo br g (O Sherwood)

Race type	NHF: 4 (0-1)
	Hdl: P657P (0-5)
	Chs: 11224P71U6 (3-10)
Conclusion:	he's best over fences.
Distance	2m-2m7.5f: 4P57P (0-5)
	3m-3m2.5f: 611247 (2-6)
	3m4f+: 2P1U6 (1-5)
Conclusion:	he needs a trip of at least 3m.
Going	Good (good to firm in places) or faster: U6 (0-2)
	Good: 1 (1-1)
	Good to soft: 2P (0-2)
	Soft: 7124P (1-5)
	Heavy: 4P6517 (1-6)
Conclusion:	his wins have come on good or softer going.
Track	Left-handed: 47141U (2-6)
	Right-handed: P65122PP76 (1-10)
Conclusion:	he has a superior strike-rate on left-handed tracks.
Fresh	First run of the season: 46P (0-3)
	Second run of the season: P74 (0-3)
	Third or subsequent runs: 61122P71U6 (3-10)
Conclusion:	he might need at least two runs before reaching peak fitness.

Summary of ideal conditions He has proved profitable to follow blindly since switched to chasing – recording wins at 8-1, 3-1 and 11-1 from just ten starts – but his record over fences improves to: 11U (2-3) if we only consider his left-handed runs on his third or subsequent start of the season.

BENETWOOD (IRE)
8yo br g (V R A Dartnall)

Race type	NHF: 1 (1-1)
	Hdl: 212152P11110 (6-12)
	Chs: 31PP5 (1-5)
Conclusion:	he scraped home by a neck at Warwick on his second chase start (2-5 favourite) but didn't really take to fences and has since been returned to hurdling.
Distance	2m-2m3f: 1212131P552P1111 (8-16)
	2m4f-2m6f: P0 (0-2)
Conclusion:	he struggles to stay beyond 2m3f.
Jockey	A P McCoy: 11131PP2P11110 (7-14)
	Others: 2255 (0-4)
Conclusion:	all his wins have come for Tony McCoy.
Track	Left-handed: 1121P51110 (6-10)
	Right-handed: 213P52P1 (2-8)
Conclusion:	he has often earned the comment 'jumped left' and has a superior strike-rate when racing left-handed.
Headgear	Blinkers: 5 (0-1)
Conclusion:	he jumped poorly before finishing a 16-length fifth of nine when tried over hurdles in blinkers.

Summary of ideal conditions When racing in bumpers or over hurdles his record without headgear stands at: 121212P11110 (7-12), improving to: 11111 (5-5) when racing left-handed for Tony McCoy at 2m-2m3f.

BERMUDA POINTE (IRE)
7yo ch g (N A Twiston-Davies)

Race type	NHF: 1 (1-1)
	Hdl: 397 (0-3)
	Chs: 1233249143321P (3-14)
Conclusion:	his recent wins have come over fences, despite some indifferent jumping.
Distance	2m-2m1f: 1131P (3-5)
	2m2f-2m5f: 9723933 (0-7)
	2m6f-2m7f: 321 (1-3)
	3m+: 442 (0-3)
Conclusion:	he stays further than 2m but has a superior strike-rate at around that trip.

Going	Good to firm or faster: 34 (0-2)
	Good: 19121P (3-6)
	Good to soft: 19324 (1-5)
	Soft: 3233 (0-4)
	Heavy: 7 (0-1)
Conclusion:	good ground is ideal for him.
Fresh	Seasonal debuts: 1311 (3-4)
	Others: 9723324943321P (1-14)
Conclusion:	he runs especially well when fresh, with three of his four wins coming first time out and the other after a break of approximately six weeks.

Summary of ideal conditions When making his seasonal debut on good to soft or faster going his record reads: 111 (3-3). Given his propensity to make jumping errors he'll be suited to racing in small fields or on tracks that claim a low percentage of fallers (e.g. Carlisle).

BERNARD

9yo b g (K Bishop)

Race type	Hdl: 0004461622PP (1-12)
	Chs: U12U5 (1-5)
Conclusion:	he's effective over hurdles and fences.
Distance	2m-2m2.5f: 00 (0-2)
	2m3f-2m5.5f: 0U6PP (0-5)
	2m6f-2m7.5f: 1225 (1-4)
	3m+: 44612U (1-6)
Conclusion:	his best efforts have come over 2m6f or further.
Going	Good to firm or faster: 1U (1-2)
	Good: 46P25 (0-5)
	Good to soft: U412 (1-4)
	Soft/heavy: 00062P (0-6)
Conclusion:	he's best on fast ground. His win on officially good to soft going at Exeter on 27 November 2007 is misleading as the ground was much faster than the official version (Raceform rated it as good to firm).
Course	Exeter: 41622PP1 (2-8)
	Stratford: U (0-1)
	Taunton: 0 (0-1)
	Uttoxeter: 462U5 (0-5)
	Warwick: 0 (0-1)
	Wincanton: 0 (0-1)
Conclusion:	he has yet to win away from Exeter.

Field size	16 or more runners: 00422 (0-5)
	12-15 runners: 0U46112 (2-7)
	11 or fewer runners: 6PPU5 (0-5)
Conclusion:	he's best coming late off a strong pace, the sort only normally produced in big fields.

Summary of ideal conditions When racing over 2m6f or further his record reads: 44612212U5 (2-10). These figures improve to: 41221 (2-5) if we only consider his 2m6f+ runs in fields of 12 or more runners at Exeter, with the fourth placing coming in an 18-runner handicap hurdle when a 33-1 shot.

BESHABAR (IRE)
7yo ch g (P F Nicholls)

Race type	Hdl: 2151 (2-4)
Conclusion:	his four runs under National Hunt Rules have taken place over hurdles but he is regarded as a potential future chase star.
Distance	2m3f-2m5f: 2151 (2-4)
Conclusion:	he is fully effective at about 2m4f but should stay 3m in time.
Going	Good: 1 (1-1)
	Good to soft: 215 (1-3)
	Soft/heavy: no runs
Conclusion:	his impressive Grade 3 Sandown win on his final start for Nick Williams came on good going but he is expected to prove best with some cut in the ground.

Summary of ideal conditions He made huge strides in just four outings for Nick Williams during the 2007-2008 season, finishing runner-up at 66-1 in a Newbury novices' hurdle before scoring at Exeter (evens) and Sandown (9-1). He missed the 2008-2009 season through injury but should make up for lost time.

BIBLE LORD (IRE)
8yo ch g (Andrew Turnell)

Race type	Hdl: 0 (0-1)
	Chs: 6211496140386FF (3-15)
Conclusion:	he's best over fences.
Distance	2m-2m2f: 0 (0-1)
	2m3f-2m5.5f: 2111438FF (3-9)
	3m+: 649606 (0-6)
Conclusion:	his best efforts have come at around 2m4f.

Going	Good or faster: 036F (0-4)
	Good to soft: 6214614F (2-8)
	Soft: 098 (0-3)
	Heavy: 1 (1-1)
Conclusion:	he is suited by good to soft or softer going.
Field size	12 or more runners: 649640386FF (0-11)
(chase runs	11 or fewer runners: 2111 (3-4)
only)	
Conclusion:	he has yet to win a big-field chase.

Summary of ideal conditions Combine chase starts with racing in fields of 11 or fewer runners and his record becomes: 2111 (3-4). All four runs took place over trips of around 2m4f on good to soft or softer going.

BIG FELLA THANKS

7yo b g (P F Nicholls)

Race type	Hdl: 112 (2-3)
	Chs: 322U136 (1-7)
Conclusion:	he's effective over hurdles and fences.
Distance	3m-3m2f: 112322U13 (3-9)
	4m+: 6 (0-1)
Conclusion:	his wins have come at about 3m but he was far from disgraced when a 23-length sixth of 40 in the 2009 Grand National (4m4f).
Going	Good to firm or faster: no runs
	Good: U3 (0-2)
	Good to soft: 26 (0-2)
	Soft: 1221 (2-4)
	Heavy: 1 (1-1)
Conclusion:	he's suited by soft or heavy going.
Track	Left-handed: 123216 (2-6)
	Right-handed: 12U3 (1-4)
Conclusion:	he jumped out to his left when beaten at odds of 1-4 in a beginners' chase at right-handed Taunton in December 2008 (albeit in first time blinkers) and might prove best left-handed.

Summary of ideal conditions Combine a distance of 3m or further with running on good to soft or softer going and his record becomes: 1122216 (3-7), improving to: 11221 (3-5) on soft or heavy ground only.

BIG ZEB (IRE)

8yo b g (C A Murphy)

Race type	NHF: 223 (0-3)
	Hdl: 1221 (2-4)
	Chs: F1F2211FF2 (3-10)
Conclusion:	he has a good record over hurdles (his only defeats were by subsequent Grade 1 winners Sizing Europe and Catch Me) and is developing into a top class chaser.
Distance	2m-2m1f: 2231211FF12 (4-11)
	2m2f-2m3f: 2F (0-2)
	2m4f-2m6f: 1F22 (1-4)
Conclusion:	he won a beginners' chase over 2m5.5f at Fairyhouse but all his other wins have come at about 2m.
Going	Good to yielding or faster: 22F11 (2-5)
	Yielding: F (0-1)
	Yielding to soft: 2221 (1-4)
	Soft: 2 (0-1)
	Soft to heavy: 311F2 (2-5)
	Heavy: F (0-1)
Conclusion:	he seems effective on any going.
Field size	12 or more runners: F1FF (1-4)
(chase runs	8-11 runners: no runs
only)	7 or fewer runners: 2211F2 (2-6)
Conclusion:	his jumping remains far from fluent and he is likely to prove best in small fields.

Summary of ideal conditions When racing at 2m-2m1f over hurdles or fences his record reads: 1211FF12 (4-8), with the latest defeat by a head.

BLUEBERRY BOY (IRE)

10yo b g (Paul Stafford)

Race type	NHF: P133 (1-4)
	Hdl: 21124000 (2-8)
	Chs: 1436FU1 (2-7)
Conclusion:	he's effective over hurdles and fences.
Going	Good to yielding or faster: 2FU00 (0-5)
	Yielding: P40 (0-3)
	Yielding to soft: 2 (0-1)
	Soft: 3111 (3-4)
	Soft to heavy: 1331 (2-4)
	Heavy: 46 (0-2)
Conclusion:	his best efforts have come on soft going.

Course	Punchestown: 2111F1 (4-6)
	Others: P133240436U00 (1-13)
Conclusion:	he runs especially well at Punchestown (his other win came at Leopardstown).

Summary of ideal conditions When racing at Punchestown his record is: 2111F1 (4-6), improving to: 1111 (4-4) on soft or heavy going.

BRIAREUS

9yo ch g (A M Balding)

Race type	Hdl: 2112016 (3-7)
	Chs: 2114FP (2-6)
Conclusion:	he is effective over hurdles and fences.
Distance	2m-2m3f: 2112016211F (5-11)
	2m4f-2m5f: P (0-1)
	3m+: 4 (0-1)
Conclusion:	all his wins have come at trips short of 2m4f.
Going	Good to firm or faster: no runs
	Good: 114P (2-4)
	Good to soft: 121621F (3-7)
	Soft/heavy: 20 (0-2)
Conclusion:	he runs best on good to soft or faster going.
Track	Flat: 11212114P (5-9)
	Significant undulations: 206F (0-4)
Conclusion:	he's best on flat tracks.
Class	Grade 1: 64FP (0-4)
	Grade 2: 11 (2-2)
	Grade 3: no runs
	Listed: 0 (0-1)
	Others: 211221 (3-6)
Conclusion:	his wins have come in Grade 2 or lower company.

Summary of ideal conditions When racing on good to soft or faster going his record is: 112162114FP (5-11), improving to: 1121211 (5-7) if we ignore his runs in Grade 1 company and those at 2m4f or further.

BRIERY FOX (IRE)

11yo ch g (H D Daly)

Race type	NHF: 1 (1-1)
	Hdl: 413 (1-3)
	Ch: 421021843B4U6222537312 (3-22)
Conclusion:	he is effective over hurdles and fences.

Going	Good or faster: 11102B4625312 (4-13)
	Good to soft: 321843U2273 (1-11)
	Soft/heavy: 44 (0-2)
Conclusion:	he runs best on fast ground.
Fresh (absence	42 days or longer: 14140213B4233 (3-13)
since last race)	28-41 days: 142512 (2-6)
	27 days or less: 328U627 (0-7)
Conclusion:	all his wins have come after breaks of at least four weeks.

Summary of ideal conditions When racing on good or faster going his record is: 11102B4625312 (4-13).

BUCK THE LEGEND (IRE)
7yo b/br g (N A Twiston-Davies)

Race type	NHF: 637 (0-3)
	Hdl: F7265262 (0-8)
	Chs: 511439PF (2-8)
Conclusion:	both his wins came over fences.
Distance	2m-2m2f: 63776 (0-5)
	2m3f-2m5.5f: 211439P (2-7)
	3m+: F25265F (0-7)
Conclusion:	his wins came at about 2m4f but he does stay further.
Going	Good to firm or faster: no runs
	Good: 725PF (0-5)
	Good to soft: 6561439 (1-7)
	Soft: 637F21 (1-6)
	Heavy: 2 (0-1)
Conclusion:	he seems happiest on good to soft or softer going.
Field size	12 or more runners: 63772652259P (0-12)
	8-11 runners: 61 (1-2)
	7 or fewer runners: F143F (1-5)
Conclusion:	his jumping remains far from fluent and he is likely to prove best in small fields.
Class	1: 439 (0-3)
	2: 76PF (0-4)
	3: F2511 (2-5)
	4 or lower: 6372526 (0-7)
Conclusion:	he has yet to win above Class 3 level.

Summary of ideal conditions Combine a distance of 2m3f or further with racing in fields of 11 or fewer runners and his record becomes: F61143F (2-7), improving to: 11 (2-2) if we discard his runs at 3m or further and those in Class 1 company.

BUSY ISIT

9yo br g (Mrs F M Shaw)

Race type	NHF: 1 (1-1)
	Hdl: 1605 (1-4)
	Chs: 315911 (3-6)
Conclusion:	he's effective over hurdles and fences.
Distance	2m-2m2f: 1 (1-1)
	2m3f-2m5f: 1031911 (4-7)
	2m5.5f-2m7f: 65 (0-2)
	3m+: 5 (0-1)
Conclusion:	2m5f seems to be the outer limit of his stamina.
Going	Good to firm or faster: 1 (1-1)
	Good: 0591 (1-4)
	Good to soft: 1511 (3-4)
	Soft: 63 (0-2)
	Heavy: no runs
Conclusion:	he's best on good to soft or faster going.
Fresh (absence since last race)	56 days or longer: 1105111 (5-7)
	42-55 days: no runs
	28-41 days: 39 (0-2)
	27 days or less: 65 (0-2)
Conclusion:	he runs especially well when fresh.
Track	Left-handed: 09 (0-2)
	Right-handed: 116531511 (5-9)
Conclusion:	he has yet to prove his effectiveness on left-handed tracks.

Summary of ideal conditions When racing on good to soft or faster going his record reads: 110515911 (5-9). These figures improve to: 11111 (5-5) if we only consider his right-handed runs when fresh (after a break of six weeks or more).

BY GEORGE (IRE)

7yo b g (N J Gifford)

Race type	NHF: 67 (0-2)
	Hdl: 5547 (0-4)
	Chs: U13253 (1-6)
Conclusion:	his sole win came over fences.
Track	Left-handed: 775 (0-3)
	Right-handed: 6544U1323 (1-9)
Conclusion:	he's best right-handed.

Headgear	Cheekpieces: 253 (0-3)
	Without headgear: 675547U13 (1-9)
Conclusion:	the application of headgear looked the obvious solution to his less-than-willing attitude but didn't have the desired effect – he earned the comment 'not run on' when a close second of 18 in first time cheekpieces at Huntingdon (19 February 2009) then jumped poorly when beaten at Newbury and Ascot.

Summary of ideal conditions When racing right-handed over hurdles or fences his record reads: 554U1323 (1-8). His jumping remains far from fluent but he could be the type to run up a sequence if returned to hurdles this term.

CAN'T BUY TIME (IRE)

7yo b g (Jonjo O'Neill)

Race type	NHF: 6 (0-1)
	Hdl: 455 (0-3)
	Chs: 363111314F (4-10)
Conclusion:	all his wins have come over fences.
Distance	2m-2m2f: 655 (0-3)
	2m3f-2m7.5f: 4363 (0-4)
	3m-3m1f: 11131 (4-5)
	4m+: 4F (0-2)
Conclusion:	he seems best at about 3m.
Going	Good to firm or faster: no runs
	Good: 54111 (3-5)
	Good to soft: 5614F (1-5)
	Soft: 533 (0-3)
	Heavy: 3 (0-1)
Conclusion:	he handles mud but seems happiest on good to soft or faster going.
Field size	12 or more runners: 64F (0-3)
(chase runs	10-11 runners: 33 (0-2)
only)	9 or fewer runners: 31111 (4-5)
Conclusion:	his chase wins have come in single-digit line-ups but his Cheltenham Festival fourth of 19 suggests that he can handle traffic.

Summary of ideal conditions When running over 3m or further his record reads: 111314F (4-7), improving to: 1111 (4-4) if we only consider his runs at 3m-3m1f on good to soft or faster going.

CAPE TRIBULATION
5yo b g (J M Jefferson)

Race type	NHF: 113 (2-3)
	Flat: 715 (1-3)
	Hdl: 11550 (2-5)
Conclusion:	he has winning form in bumpers, on the Flat and over hurdles.
Going	Good or faster: 350 (0-3)
	Good (good to soft in places): 1 (1-1)
	Good to soft: 17155 (2-5)
	Soft/heavy: 11 (2-2)
Conclusion:	the softer the going, the better he runs.
Track	Flat: 113151150 (5-9)
	Significant undulations: 75 (0-2)
Conclusion:	he ran poorly on the Flat at Pontefract and over jumps at Cheltenham but both runs came on good to soft going (barely slow enough for him) and it's too early to say that he is only effective on flat tracks.

Summary of ideal conditions When racing on ground slower than good his record reads: 11711155 (5-8), improving to: 11 (2-2) on soft or heavy going only.

CARRICKBOY (IRE)
5yo b g (Miss Venetia Williams)

Race type	NHF: 3 (0-1)
	Hdl: 2S11704 (2-7)
Conclusion:	both his wins came over hurdles but he should make a chaser in time.
Distance	2m-2m2f: 3S117 (2-5)
	2m3f-2m5f: 204 (0-3)
Conclusion:	he is likely to prove best at about 2m.
Going	Good to firm or faster: no runs
	Good: 24 (0-2)
	Good to soft: 370 (0-3)
	Soft: 1 (1-1)
	Heavy: S1 (1-2)
Conclusion:	he is suited by soft or heavy going.

Summary of ideal conditions When racing from 2m-2m2f his record reads: 3S117 (2-5), improving to: S11 (2-3) on soft or heavy going, with the sole defeat excusable as he stumbled and unseated his jockey before the first flight at Towcester.

CARRUTHERS
6yo b g (M Bradstock)

Race type	NHF: 2 (0-1)
	Hdl: 12110 (3-5)
	Chs: 2114 (2-4)
Conclusion:	he's effective over hurdles and fences.
Distance	2m-2m2f: 2 (0-1)
	2m3f-2m6f: 121 (2-3)
	3m+: 102114 (3-6)
Conclusion:	he needs at least 2m3f.
Going	Good to firm or faster: no runs
	Good: 21 (1-2)
	Good to soft: 104 (1-3)
	Soft: 212 (1-3)
	Heavy: 11 (2-2)
Conclusion:	his good-ground win came when 2-11 favourite at Fakenham and he's likely to prove best in the mud.
Course	Ascot: 1 (1-1)
	Bangor: 1 (1-1)
	Cheltenham: 04 (0-2)
	Chepstow: 1 (1-1)
	Exeter: 2 (0-1)
	Fakenham: 1 (1-1)
	Uttoxeter: 22 (0-2)
	Warwick: 1 (1-1)
Conclusion:	he has twice disappointed at Cheltenham, though both runs came in Grade 1 company and on ground plenty quick enough for him.
Fresh	Seasonal debuts: 22 (0-2)
Conclusion:	he might need his first run of the season.

Summary of ideal conditions When racing over hurdles or fences his record reads: 121102114 (5-9), improving to: 1211211 (5-7) if we discard his runs at Cheltenham.

CATCH ME (GER)
7yo br g (E J O'Grady)

Race type	Hdl: 112U3F1416511115 (8-16)
Conclusion:	he has a 50% strike-rate over hurdles.
Distance	2m-2m2f: 112U1416 (4-8)
	2m3f-2m5f: 3F1115 (3-6)
	3m+: 51 (1-2)
Conclusion:	he was all out to win by a head over 3m at Leopardstown on 28 December 2008 (4-6 favourite) and is likely to prove best over shorter trips.
Going	Good or faster: F45 (0-3)
	Yielding (or good to soft): 3615 (1-4)
	Yielding to soft: 11 (2-2)
	Soft: 1111 (4-4)
	Heavy: 2U1 (1-3)
Conclusion:	the softer the going, the better he runs.

Summary of ideal conditions When racing on yielding to soft or softer going his record reads: 112U11111 (7-9), with the runner-up effort by a neck. All the wins came over 2m-2m5f.

CHARACTER BUILDING (IRE)
9yo gr g (J J Quinn)

Race type	NHF: 322 (0-3)
	Hdl: 24113 (2-5)
	Chs: 21412P34391 (3-11)
Conclusion:	he's effective over hurdles and fences.
Distance	2m-2m2f: 322 (0-3)
	2m3f-2m6f: 24124113 (3-8)
	3m-3m2f110y: 13431 (2-5)
	3m4f: 9 (0-1)
	4m+: 2P (0-2)
Conclusion:	he's suited by a test of stamina.
Going	Good to firm or faster: 1P (1-2)
	Good: 22 (0-2)
	Good to soft: 21431 (2-5)
	Soft: 322411339 (2-9)
	Heavy: 4 (0-1)
Conclusion:	his fast-ground win came in a weak race at Sedgefield and he is likely to prove best on slower going.

Course	Ayr: 24P (0-3)
	Catterick: 2 (0-1)
	Cheltenham: 42431 (1-5)
	Doncaster: 3 (0-1)
	Haydock: 9 (0-1)
	Market Rasen: 1 (1-1)
	Newbury: 3 (0-1)
	Newcastle: 2 (0-1)
	Sedgefield: 321 (1-3)
	Towcester: 1 (1-1)
	Warwick: 1 (1-1)
Conclusion:	he won weak events at Market Rasen and Warwick but his other wins have come on tracks with steep uphill finishes (e.g. Cheltenham and Towcester).

Summary of ideal conditions When racing on good or softer going his record over obstacles stands at: 24214123143391 (4-14), with the sole out-of-the-frame effort excusable as he didn't take to first time cheekpieces at Haydock.

CHARMAINE WOOD
6yo b m (A King)

Race type	NHF: 217 (1-3)
	Hdl: 1147P (2-5)
Conclusion:	she has a 40% strike-rate over hurdles.
Track	Left-handed: 747P (0-4)
	Right-handed: 2111 (3-4)
Conclusion:	she has yet to prove her effectiveness on left-handed tracks.

Summary of ideal conditions When racing right-handed her record reads: 2111 (3-4), with the sole defeat coming in a Sandown bumper on her racecourse debut. All her wins came at 2m on good or softer going.

CLOUDY LANE
9yo b g (D McCain Jnr)

Race type	NHF: 21 (1-2)
	Hdl: F21121 (3-6)
	Chs: 361201U511169431FU (6-18)
Conclusion:	he has winning form over hurdles and fences.

Distance	2m-2m2f: 21F (1-3)
	2m3f-2m6.5f: 2111369F (3-8)
	3m-3m1f: 2121511431 (5-10)
	3m2f: 1 (1-1)
	3m4f+: 0U6U (0-4)
Conclusion:	he has proved disappointing when tried over extreme trips and is likely to prove best at around the 3m-3m2f mark.
Going	Good or faster: 13U16 (2-5)
	Good to soft: F21614U (2-7)
	Soft: 211251931F (4-10)
	Heavy: 2101 (2-4)
Conclusion:	he seems happiest on good to soft or softer going.
Fresh	Seasonal debuts: 2F359 (0-5)
	Second run: 12614 (2-5)
	Third or subsequent runs: 11211201U11631FU (8-16)
Conclusion:	he has yet to win first time out.
Course	Aintree (Grand National): 6U (0-2)
	Aintree (Mildmay): 39 (0-2)
	Ayr: 1 (1-1)
	Bangor: 26 (0-2)
	Cheltenham: 1 (1-1)
	Doncaster: 1 (1-1)
	Fairyhouse: U (0-1)
	Haydock: 11105141 (5-8)
	Hexham: F (0-1)
	Kelso: F (0-1)
	Newcastle: 12 (1-2)
	Sedgefield: 2 (0-1)
	Southwell: 1 (1-1)
	Uttoxeter: 2 (0-1)
	Wetherby: 3 (0-1)
Conclusion:	he seems best on galloping tracks.

Summary of ideal conditions When racing over hurdles or fences at 2m4f or further his record becomes: 21121361201U511169431FU (9-23), improving to: 2111121111431 (9-13) if we throw out his runs on tight tracks and those at 3m4f or further. He has been beaten in the last two Grand Nationals – finishing a 33-length sixth in 2008 before unseating his rider the following year – and hopefully his connections will accept that he lacks the size and stamina for the race.

COE (IRE)

7yo br g (Mrs S J Smith)

Race type	NHF: 544 (0-3)
	Hdl: 5311230 (2-7)
	Chs: 53412F9 (1-7)
Conclusion:	he's effective over hurdles and fences.
Distance	1m4f-2m2f: 544 (0-3)
	2m3f-2m5f: 53154 (1-5)
	2m6f-2m7f: 13 (1-2)
	3m+: 23012F9 (1-7)
Conclusion:	he improved for the return to 3m+ last season, scoring over 3m4f at Haydock.
Going	Good or faster: 5259 (0-4)
	Good to soft: 330F (0-4)
	Soft: 131 (2-3)
	Heavy: 544142 (1-6)
Conclusion:	he needs soft or heavy going.
Track	Left-handed: 54511230512F9 (3-13)
	Right-handed: 4334 (0-4)
Conclusion:	he jumped out to his left when disappointing at right-handed Market Rasen last term and is likely to prove best left-handed.

Summary of ideal conditions Combine a distance of 2m3f or further with racing on soft or heavy going and his record becomes: 113412 (3-6), improving to: 1112 (3-4) on left-handed tracks only.

CONSIGLIERE (FR)

6yo ch g (D E Pipe)

Race type	Chs: 4633151110 (4-10)
Conclusion:	he won over hurdles in France and has a 40% strike-rate over fences since arriving in the UK.
Distance	2m-2m2f: 63311 (2-5)
	2m3f-2m4f: 511 (2-3)
	2m5f-2m6f: 40 (0-2)
Conclusion:	his wins have come from 2m-2m4f.
Going	Good to firm or faster: no runs
	Good: 6350 (0-4)
	Good to soft: 3 (0-1)
	Soft: 4111 (3-4)
	Heavy: 1 (1-1)
Conclusion:	he prefers soft or heavy going.

Headgear	Blinkers: 3151110 (4-7)
	Without headgear: 463 (0-3)
Conclusion:	he improved for the application of headgear.
Field size	12 or more runners: 460 (0-3)
	8-11 runners: 35 (0-2)
	7 or fewer runners: 31111 (4-5)
Conclusion:	he has yet to win in a big field.

Summary of ideal conditions When wearing blinkers his record reads: 3151110 (4-7), improving to: 31111 (4-5) in fields of seven or fewer runners.

COPPER BLEU (IRE)

7yo b g (P J Hobbs)

Race type	Ptp: 61 (1-2)
	NHF: 15 (1-2)
	Hdl: 312421 (2-6)
Conclusion:	he won a maiden point-to-point in March 2007 and has since made his mark in bumpers and over hurdles.
Distance	2m-2m2f: 151241 (3-6)
	2m4f-2m5f: 32 (0-2)
Conclusion:	his wins under Rules have come at about 2m but he stays further.
Going	Good or faster: 5 (0-1)
	Good to soft: 1242 (1-4)
	Soft: 3 (0-1)
	Soft to heavy: 1 (1-1)
	Heavy: 1 (1-1)
Conclusion:	he's suited by soft or heavy going.
Course	Aintree (Mildmay): 532 (0-3)
	Cheltenham: 4 (0-1)
	Cork: 1 (1-1)
	Doncaster: 2 (0-1)
	Newbury: 1 (1-1)
	Punchestown: 1 (1-1)
Conclusion:	he has drawn a blank from three tries on Aintree's Mildmay course, though was only beaten by a head over 2m4f in a Grade 2 contest on his latest course visit.

Summary of ideal conditions Since finishing sixth in a point-to-point on his racecourse debut his record reads: 115312421 (4-9), improving to: 1112421 (4-7) if we discard his 2m runs at Aintree.

CORNAS (NZ)
7yo b g (Nick Williams)

Race type	NHF: 76 (0-2)
	Hdl: 5512458 (1-7)
	Chs: 1274 (1-4)
Conclusion:	he showed some ability in bumpers when with Evan Williams and has proved profitable to follow blind for Nick Williams, winning at 12-1 and 7-1 from eleven starts.
Distance	2m-2m1f: 7655124581274 (2-13)
Conclusion:	all his runs have come over trips of about 2m.
Going	Good to firm or faster: no runs
	Good: 75125 (1-5)
	Good to soft: 68274 (0-5)
	Soft: 541 (1-3)
	Heavy: no runs
Conclusion:	he has yet to race on extremes of going.
Track	Left-handed: 72874 (0-5)
	Right-handed: 65514512 (2-8)
Conclusion:	he has yet to win on a left-handed track, though was not disgraced in top company at the Cheltenham and Aintree Festivals last term.

Summary of ideal conditions When racing over hurdles or fences his record reads: 55124581274 (2-11), improving to: 5514512 (2-7) on right-handed tracks, with the latest defeat by a neck in Grade 2 company.

CRESCENT ISLAND (IRE)
6yo b g (N A Twiston-Davies)

Race type	NHF: 1R6 (1-3)
	Hdl: 13221 (2-5)
	Chs: R313423P (1-8)
Conclusion:	he's effective over hurdles and fences.
Distance	2m-2m2f: 1R6123 (2-6)
	2m3f-2m5.5f: 321R123 (2-7)
	3m+: 34P (0-3)
Conclusion:	he struggles to stay 3m.
Going	Good to firm or faster: no runs
	Good: 1R21312 (3-7)
	Good to soft: 3R43P (0-5)
	Soft: 6123 (1-4)
	Heavy: no runs
Conclusion:	the majority of his wins have come on good going.

Field size	12 or more runners: 13113P (3-6)
	11 or fewer runners: 1R622R3342 (1-10)
Conclusion:	he seems to lose interest if he has nothing to race with and is suited by big fields. His only small-field win came when 13-8 favourite for a nine-runner bumper at Folkestone where he earned the comment 'idled in front' from the *Racing Post*.

Summary of ideal conditions Combine a distance of 2m-2m5.5f with racing in big fields (12 or more runners) and his record becomes: 13113 (3-5), with the latest defeat coming in the 20-runner Jewson Novices' Handicap Chase at the Cheltenham festival where he raced freely in first-time blinkers (25-1).

CRUCHAIN (IRE)

6yo ch g (J J O'Neill)

Race type	NHF: 047 (0-3)
	Hdl: 2217310 (2-7)
	Chs: P1 (1-2)
Conclusion:	he's effective over hurdles and fences.
Distance	2m-2m2f: 0472213 (1-7)
	2m3f-2m6f: 710P1 (2-5)
Conclusion:	he's effective at 2m but is likely to prove best over further.
Going	Good or faster: 047P (0-4)
	Good to soft: 2271 (1-4)
	Soft/heavy: 1301 (2-4)
Conclusion:	he needs good to soft or softer going.
Fresh (absence since last race)	56 days or longer: 077P (0-4)
	43-55 days: 0 (0-1)
	28-42 days: 42131 (2-5)
	27 days or less: 21 (1-2)
Conclusion:	he has yet to run well when returning from a break of more than six weeks.

Summary of ideal conditions Combine hurdle or chase starts with running on good to soft or softer going and his record becomes: 22173101 (3-8), improving to: 221311 (3-6) after a relatively recent outing (six weeks or less since his latest one).

DARKNESS
10yo ch g (C R Egerton)

Race type	NHF: 31 (1-2)
	Hdl: 21210 (2-5)
	Chs: 121113P3P10 (5-11)
Conclusion:	he's effective over hurdles and fences.
Going	Good or faster: 301113P1 (4-8)
	Good to soft: 130 (1-3)
	Soft: 121212P (3-7)
	Heavy: no runs
Conclusion:	his soft-ground wins came in weak races – when 15-8 favourite for a bumper and when odds-on for novices hurdles at Plumpton and Towcester – and he is likely to prove best on good to soft or faster going.
Headgear	Blinkers: 0 (0-1)
	Cheekpieces: 0 (0-1)
Conclusion:	he has twice disappointed when wearing headgear, though both runs came in valuable races.
Jockey	A P McCoy: 11111P1 (6-7)
	Others: 312202133P0 (2-11)
Conclusion:	he has an excellent strike-rate for Tony McCoy.

Summary of ideal conditions If we ignore his chase runs on soft or heavy going and his two runs in headgear his record becomes: 31212111113P31 (8-14), improving to: 11111P1 (6-7) when ridden by A P McCoy.

DEEP PURPLE
8yo b g (Evan Williams)

Race type	Hdl: 1111129 (5-7)
	Chs: 411P2121 (4-8)
Conclusion:	he's effective over hurdles and fences.
Distance	2m-2m2f: 11112941P21 (6-11)
	2m3f-2m4f: 1121 (3-4)
Conclusion:	he has winning form from 2m-2m4f.
Going	Good to firm or faster: 114 (2-3)
	Good: 111P2121 (5-8)
	Good to soft: 911 (2-3)
	Soft: 2 (0-1)
	Heavy: no runs
Conclusion:	he's suited by fast going.

Track	Left-handed: 119421 (3-6)
	Right-handed: 111211P21 (6-9)

Conclusion: although a multiple winner on right-handed tracks he tends to jump out to his left and might prove best on left-handed courses.

Field size	12 or more runners: 9 (0-1)
	8-11 runners: 112412 (3-6)
	7 or fewer runners: 1111P211 (6-8)

Conclusion: he's a front-runner and is best able to dominate in small fields.

Summary of ideal conditions When racing over hurdles or fences on good to soft or faster going his record reads: 111119411P2121 (9-14).

DEFINITY (IRE)

6yo b/br g (P F Nicholls)

Race type	Ptp: 1 (1-1)
	Hdl: 112 (2-3)

Conclusion: he won a maiden point-to-point in Ireland and proved most progressive over hurdles in his first season for Paul Nicholls.

Distance	2m5f-2m6f: 1 (1-1)
	3m+: 112 (2-3)

Conclusion: he was unimpressive when dropped to 2m6f on a tight track for his winning hurdles debut and is likely to prove best over 3m or further.

Going	Good to firm or faster: no runs
	Good: 11 (2-2)
	Good to soft: 12 (1-2)
	Soft/heavy no runs

Conclusion: he has yet to race on extremes of going.

Summary of ideal conditions Quite simply, he has yet to run a bad race, recording figures of: 1112 (3-4), with the sole defeat by three-quarters of a length after hanging badly at Cheltenham. There should be further improvement to come when he returns to fences.

DIZZY FUTURE
7yo b g (Mrs Caroline Keevil)

Race type	Hdl: 97257313500117P66P16 (4-20)
	Chs: 112P (2-4)
Conclusion:	he's effective over hurdles and fences.
Distance	2m-2m2f: 977 (0-3)
	2m3f-2m5.5f: 25350 (0-5)
	2m6f-2m7f: 10P (1-3)
	3m+: 311766P11126P (5-13)
Conclusion:	all bar one of his wins came over 3m or further.
Time of year	Jan: P (0-1)
	Feb: no runs
	Mar: 00 (0-2)
	Apr: 711112 (4-6)
	May: 2516 (1-4)
	Jun: 7 (0-1)
	Jul: 7PP (0-3)
	Aug: 3 (0-1)
	Sep: 136 (1-3)
	Oct: 96 (0-2)
	Nov: no runs
	Dec: 5 (0-1)
Conclusion:	he tends to peak in the spring.

Summary of ideal conditions When running in April or May his record reads: 7251111126 (5-10), improving to: 1111126 (5-7) over distances of 3m or further. All his wins came on good or faster going.

DOM D'ORGEVAL (FR)
9yo b g (D E Pipe)

Race type	NHF: 08 (0-2)
	Hdl: 069P6111221253251113543435 (7-26)
	Chs: 1103PP7P (2-8)
Conclusion:	he landed his first two starts over fences but those wins came in tiny fields at gaff tracks (Fakenham and Hexham) and he has since struggled over the larger obstacles.
Distance	1m4f-1m5f: 08 (0-2)
	2m-2m1f: 0691121525 (3-10)
	2m3f-2m5f110y: 612231113435 (4-12)
	2m6f+: P5431103PP7P (2-12)
Conclusion:	his 2m wins came early in his career and he seems to need at least 2m4f these days.

Going	Good to firm or faster: 01 (1-2)
	Good: 0P61222353 (1-10)
	Good to soft: 953510P5 (1-8)
	Soft/heavy: 8611211143431PP7 (6-16)
Conclusion:	he would appear effective on any ground but has a particularly good record on soft or heavy going.
Track	Left-handed: 06P6111221253251113543431103PP75 (9-32)
	Right-handed: 809P (0-4)
Conclusion:	he has yet to win on a right-handed track.
Class (hurdle runs only)	Handicaps: 069654343 (0-9)
	Non-handicaps: P1112212532511135 (7-17)
Conclusion:	he has a good record in handicap hurdles.
Headgear	Blinkers: P (0-1)
	Cheekpieces: 5 (0-1)
	Visor: P (0-1)
Conclusion:	he has yet to win in headgear.

Summary of ideal conditions His record in handicap hurdles reads: P1112212532511135 (7-17), improving to: 112311135 (5-9) at 2m4f or further (or at shorter trips on soft/heavy going).

DUC DE REGNIERE (FR)

7yo b g (N J Henderson)

Race type	Hdl: 110112355 (4-9)
	Chs: 312 (1-3)
Conclusion:	he didn't take to fences, his sole win coming when 2-7 favourite.
Fresh	First run of the season: 131 (2-3)
	Second run of the season: 111 (3-3)
	Third or subsequent runs: 022355 (0-6)
Conclusion:	he tends to peak early in the season.

Summary of ideal conditions When only considering his first two runs each season his record becomes: 113111 (5-6), improving to: 1111 (4-4) over hurdles only.

EARTH PLANET (IRE)
6yo b g (P F Nicholls)

Race type	NHF: 123 (1-3)
	Hdl: 25261143 (2-8)
Conclusion:	he has reached a place in nine of his 11 career starts (the fourth placing came in a 17-runner handicap).
Distance	2m-2m2f110y: 123 (1-3)
	2m3f-2m5f110y: 2521143 (2-7)
	2m6f+: 6 (0-1)
Conclusion:	his best efforts have come at about 2m4f but he might stay further.
Going	Good to firm or faster: no runs
	Good: 143 (1-3)
	Good to soft: 225261 (1-6)
	Soft: 31 (1-2)
	Heavy: no runs
Conclusion:	he has yet to race on extremes of going.
Field size	12 or more runners: 1256114 (3-7)
	11 or fewer runners: 2323 (0-4)
Conclusion:	his three wins came in big fields.
Track	Left-handed: 135613 (2-6)
	Right-handed: 22214 (1-5)
Conclusion:	he has winning form on both left-handed and right-handed tracks.
Headgear	Tongue-tie: 1143 (2-4)
	Without: 1232526 (1-7)
Conclusion:	he improved when a tongue-tie was fitted.
Jockey	Ruby Walsh: 121143 (3-6)
	Others: 32526 (0-5)
Conclusion:	all his wins came when ridden by Ruby Walsh.

Summary of ideal conditions When racing in fields of 12 or more runners his record reads: 1256114 (3-7), improving to: 1114 (3-4) when ridden by Ruby Walsh.

EL DANCER (GER)
5yo b g (Mrs L Wadham)

Race type	Hdl: 62116 (2-5)
Conclusion:	he has a 40% strike-rate over hurdles and should make a decent chaser this term.
Track	Left-handed: 611 (2-3)
	Right-handed: 26 (0-2)
Conclusion:	he has earned comments such as 'jumped left' and 'edged left' and might prove best left-handed.

Fresh   Seasonal debut: 6 (0-1)
Conclusion: he might need his first run of the season.
Summary of ideal conditions Aside from seasonal debuts, his record left-handed reads: 11 (2-2), with the wins coming on sharp tracks and on good or softer going.

ELZAHANN (IRE)

7yo b m (Ferdy Murphy)

Race type	NHF: 1 (1-1)
	Hdl: 01232111 (4-8)
Conclusion:	she has a 50% strike-rate over hurdles.
Distance	2m-2m2f: 10 (1-2)
	2m3f-2m5f: 1232 (1-4)
	3m+: 111 (3-3)
Conclusion:	she's unbeaten over 3m or further.
Going	Good or faster: 112111 (5-6)
	Good to soft: 3 (0-1)
	Soft/heavy: 02 (0-2)
Conclusion:	she's best on good or faster going.
Time of year	Jan: 3 (0-1)
	Feb: no runs
	Mar: 12 (1-2)
	Apr: 11 (2-2)
	May: 1 (1-1)
	Jun-Oct: no runs
	Nov: 0 (0-1)
	Dec: 12 (1-2)
Conclusion:	she has a good record in the spring.

Summary of ideal conditions When racing on good or faster going her record reads: 112111 (5-6), with the sole defeat by a neck when running over an inadequate 2m4f trip.

ENGLISHTOWN (FR)
9yo b g (J J O'Neill)

Race type	Hdl: 924641312025300011 (4-18)
	Chs: 321U24160P (2-10)
Conclusion:	his jumping remains far from fluent and he might prove best over hurdles.
Going	Good to firm or faster: 921121P0 (3-8)
	Good: 4632146025001 (2-13)
	Good to soft: 4023 (0-4)
	Soft: 3U1 (1-3)
	Heavy: no runs
Conclusion:	his soft-ground win came in a weak four-runner affair at Worcester and he is likely to prove best on a fast surface.
Headgear	Blinkers: 6 (0-1)
	Cheekpieces: 011 (2-3)
	Without headgear: 924341312021U24160P25300 (4-24)
Conclusion:	he has won two of his three starts in cheekpieces.
Track	Left-handed: 26341312024160P2530011 (5-22)
	Right-handed: 9421U0 (1-6)
Conclusion:	he has jumped out to his left on occasions and is likely to prove best on left-handed tracks.

Summary of ideal conditions Combine left-handed handicap hurdle starts with racing on good or faster going and his record becomes: 6131223001 (3-10).

FINGER ONTHE PULSE (IRE)
8yo b g (T J Taafe)

Race type	NHF: 1 (1-1)
	Hdl: F221312110UF (4-12)
	Chs: 3F2215123U60 (2-12)
Conclusion:	he is effective over hurdles and fences.
Distance	2m-2m2f: 1F22111U (4-8)
	2m3f-2m5.5f: 32110UF3F2212360 (3-16)
	3m+: 5 (0-1)
Conclusion:	he seems best at 2m-2m5f.

Going	Good to firm: F (0-1)

Going
Good to firm: F (0-1)
Good: 50 (0-2)
Good to yielding: F23 (0-3)
Yielding: 21U16 (2-5)
Yielding to soft: 313 (1-3)
Soft: 1012 (2-4)
Soft to heavy: 112 (2-3)
Heavy: 2F2U (0-4)
Conclusion: he seems effective on most going types.
Fresh First two runs each season or after a break of five weeks+:
1F21110U3F151236 (6-16)
Others: 2132F22U0 (1-9)
Conclusion: he runs especially well when fresh.
Time of year Mar-Oct: F1211UF15160 (5-12)
Nov-Feb: 1221303F2223U (2-13)
Conclusion: the majority of his wins have come outside the winter months.
Summary of ideal conditions When racing over trips short of 3m his record reads:
1F221312110UF3F221123U60 (7-24), improving to: F111116 (5-7) when running
fresh from March to October.

FIRE AND RAIN (FR)
6yo b g (Miss E C Lavelle)
Race type Hdl: 3644 (0-4)
Chs: UP111317 (4-8)
Conclusion: he has won four of his five completed chase starts.
Going Good or faster: 34U111317 (4-9)
Good to soft: 64P (0-3)
Soft/heavy: no runs
Conclusion: all his wins have come on good or faster going.
Track Left-handed: 317 (1-3)
Right-handed: 764UP1113 (3-9)
Conclusion: he won three times on right-handed tracks in the spring of 2009
but he jumped out to his left on each occasion.
Summary of ideal conditions When racing over fences his record reads:
UP111317 (4-8), improving to: U111317 (4-7) on good or faster going, with all four
wins coming in spring/summer from 2m4f-3m4f.

FIRST LOOK (FR)
9yo b g (P Monteith)

Race type	Hdl: 2312152685 (2-10)
	Chs: 31302341U4316P82 (3-16)
Conclusion:	he's effective over hurdles and fences.
Distance	2m-2m2f: 2312521U64285 (2-13)
	2m3f-2m4f: 131023416 (3-9)
	2m4.5f-2m6f: 38 (0-2)
	3m+: 3P (0-2)
Conclusion:	he struggles to stay beyond 2m4f.
Course	Ayr: 21123411P2 (4-10)
	Others: 31253302U6436885 (1-16)
Conclusion:	he's an Ayr course expert. His only other win came in a maiden hurdle at Kelso back in December 2005.

Summary of ideal conditions Combine a distance of 2m-2m4f with running at Ayr and his record becomes: 211234112 (4-9).

FLAKE
9yo ch g (Mrs S J Smith)

Race type	Hdl: 322587234370514911748134994234 (4-30)
	Chs: 1222532115U4419270913 (5-21)
Conclusion:	he's effective over hurdles and fences.
Field size	12 or more runners: 322430591U78944 (1-15)
	10-11 runners: 5877541499093 (1-13)
	8-9 runners: 2121423473 (2-10)
	7 or fewer runners: 3221321541112 (5-13)
Conclusion:	he's a front-runner and is best able to dominate when racing in small fields.

Summary of ideal conditions When running in fields of seven or fewer runners his record reads: 3221321541112 (5-13), with the wins coming at odds of 11-1, 4-1, 4-1, 3-1 and 5-4.

FORPADYDEPLASTERER (IRE)

7yo b g (Thomas Cooper)

Race type	NHF: 1 (1-1)
	Hdl: 1214 (2-4)
	Chs: 122212 (2-6)
Conclusion:	he's a Grade 1 winner over hurdles and fences.
Distance	2m-2m2f: 11211212 (5-8)
	2m3f-2m5f: 422 (0-3)
Conclusion:	all his wins have come at about 2m.
Field size	16 or more runners: 1111 (4-4)
	12-15 runners: 4 (0-1)
	10-11 runners: no runs
	9 or fewer runners: 212222 (1-6)
Conclusion:	the majority of his wins have come in big fields.

Summary of ideal conditions He rarely runs a bad race, recording figures of: 11214122212 (5-11) but his record can be improved to: 11411 (4-5) if we only consider his outings in fields of 12 or more runners, with the sole defeat coming in the 2008 Ballymore Properties Novices' Hurdle at the Cheltenham festival.

FORTUNATE DAVE (USA)

10yo b g (Michael Smith)

Distance	2m-2m2f110y: 17232420 (1-8)
	2m3f-2m5f110y: 830P230 (0-7)
	2m6f-2m7f: 11361 (3-5)
	3m+: 973 (0-3)
Conclusion:	he's best at around 2m6f.
Going	Good to firm or faster: 3133 (1-4)
	Good: 132428290130617 (3-15)
	Good to soft: 70P (0-3)
	Soft: 2 (0-1)
	Heavy: no runs
Conclusion:	he is suited by good or faster going.
Headgear	Cheekpieces: 113306173 (3-9)
	Visor: P (0-2)
Conclusion:	he has a good record in cheekpieces.
Course	Huntingdon: 22 (0-2)
	Market Rasen: 11313 (3-5)
Conclusion:	he has yet to run a bad race at Market Rasen or Huntingdon, both easy right-handed tracks.

Summary of ideal conditions When wearing cheekpieces his record is: 113306173 (3-9), improving to: 11313 (3-5) at Market Rasen only.

FRONTIER DANCER (IRE)

5yo b g (N A Twiston-Davies)

Race type	NHF: 41 (1-2)
	Hdl: 41F5201 (2-7)
Conclusion:	he has a 33% strike-rate to date.
Distance	2m-2m2f: 4141F21 (3-7)
	2m3f-2m5f: 50 (0-2)
Conclusion:	he has yet to prove that he can stay beyond 2m.
Going	Good to firm or faster: no runs
	Good: 41201 (2-5)
	Good to soft: 4F (0-2)
	Soft: 15 (1-2)
	Heavy: no runs
Conclusion:	he has yet to race on extremes of going.
Track	Left-handed: 411F20 (2-6)
	Right-handed: 451 (1-3)
Conclusion:	he hasn't always looked at home on right-handed tracks though he did win at Perth in April 2009.

Summary of ideal conditions When racing at 2m-2m2f his record reads: 4141F21 (3-7). From left-to-right: 4th – in need of the experience when beaten by just over nine lengths in a Uttoxeter bumper, 1st – made all the running to land a weak Uttoxeter bumper, 4th – displayed signs of greenness (keen, hung left) when fourth of 14 on his hurdles debut at right-handed Perth, 1st – accounted for 17 rivals on soft going at Warwick, F – still travelling strongly and likely to have been placed at worst had he not tipped up two from home at Cheltenham, 2nd – 17 lengths clear of the third when beaten by just over a length at Bangor, and 1st – scored by over four lengths at Perth despite hanging under pressure.

FUNDAMENTALIST (IRE)

11yo b g (N A Twiston-Davies)

Race type	Hdl: 1210 (2-4)
	Chs: 112U4FF2056P2412183F887146P6PP0 (5-31)
Conclusion:	he's effective over hurdles and fences.
Going	Good to firm or faster: 1 (1-1)
	Good: 121112UF0P24F8746 (4-17)
	Good to soft: 202183816PPP0 (2-13)
	Soft: 46 (0-2)
	Heavy: F5 (0-2)
Conclusion:	he needs good to soft or faster going.

Field size	12 or more runners: FP283F88746P6PP0 (0-16)
(chase runs	10-11 runners: 061 (1-3)
only)	8-9 runners: 51 (1-2)
	7 or fewer runners: 112U4F2412 (3-10)
Conclusion:	he has an abysmal record in big-field chases and even his 10-runner win (at Wincanton) came in a race in which only six finished.

Summary of ideal conditions When racing over hurdles or in small-field chases (10 or fewer runners) his record on good to soft or faster going becomes: 121112U241211 (7-13). He's in the twilight of his career but could run up a sequence if switched back to hurdles, a trick his trainer pulled off successfully with the 11-year-old Redemption who landed a Grade 2 contest on his reappearance in the 2007/2008 season.

GARDE CHAMPETRE (FR)
10yo b g (E Bolger)

Race type	Hurdle: 21225194 (2-8)
	Regulation chase: 245012229P (1-10)
	Cross-country chase: F1112111 (6-8)
Conclusion:	the majority of his wins have come in cross-country races.
Jockey	Nina Carberry: 111411P1 (6-8)
	Others: 2122512450122299F2 (3-18)
Conclusion:	he has an excellent strike-rate when ridden by Nina Carberry.

Summary of ideal conditions When competing in cross-country races his record reads: F1112111 (6-8), improving to: 111111 (6-6) for Nina Carberry.

GAUVAIN (GER)
7yo b g (C J Mann)

Race type	Hdl: 32221350 (1-8)
	Chs: 521F16P11 (4-9)
Conclusion:	he's best over fences.
Field size	12 or more runners: 6 (0-1)
(chase starts	8-11 runners: 52P (0-3)
only)	7 or fewer runners: 1F111 (4-5)
Conclusion:	his jumping remains far from foot-perfect and he's likely to prove best in small fields.

Summary of ideal conditions Combine chase starts with racing in fields of seven or fewer runners and his record becomes: 1F111 (4-5).

GREEN GAMBLE
9yo gr g (Mrs D M Grissell)

Race type	NHF: 0 (0-1)
	Hdl: 76403220438P (0-12)
	Chs: 12523P5855P21116126P (5-20)
Conclusion:	he is best over fences.
Distance	1m5f: 0 (0-1)
	2m-2m1.5f: 60322431523P88P5P111616P (5-24)
	2m2f-2m3f: 74522 (0-5)
	2m4f+: 025 (0-3)
Conclusion:	he seems best at 2m-2m1f.
Going	Good to firm or faster: 715388 (1-6)
	Good: 4032422P5P552112P (2-17)
	Good to soft: 23P1166 (2-7)
	Soft: 60 (0-2)
	Heavy: 7 (0-1)
Conclusion:	he seems best on good to soft or faster going.
Headgear	Blinkers: 5 (0-1)
Conclusion:	he ran poorly when tried in blinkers.

Summary of ideal conditions Combine chase starts of 2m-2m1.5f with good to soft or faster going, when not wearing headgear, and his record becomes: 1523P85P111616P (5-15). All the wins came in fields of 11 or fewer runners and he seems best on sharp tracks such as Folkestone and Lingfield.

GREENBRIDGE (IRE)
7yo b g (A King)

Race type	NHF: 2189 (1-4)
	Hdl: P23116 (2-6)
	Chs: 232P11F (2-7)
Conclusion:	he's effective over hurdles and fences.
Distance	2m-2m2.5f: 2189211623PF (3-12)
	2m3f-2m5f: P321 (1-4)
	2m6f+: 1 (1-1)
Conclusion:	he's effective over a variety of trips.
Going	Good or faster: 9P316211F (3-9)
	Good to soft: 213 (1-3)
	Soft: 2182P (1-5)
	Heavy: no runs
Conclusion:	he's best on fast going.

Course	Aintree (Mildmay): 9P6 (0-3)
	Bangor: 2 (0-1)
	Doncaster: 12 (1-2)
	Exeter: 3 (0-1)
	Fontwell: 11 (2-2)
	Hereford: 2 (0-1)
	Kempton: 12 (1-2)
	Ludlow: F (0-1)
	Newbury: 8P (0-2)
	Taunton: 13 (1-2)
Conclusion:	he runs well on sharp tracks.
Fresh	Seasonal debuts: 2P2 (0-3)
Conclusion:	he might need his first run of the season.
Time of year	Jan-Feb: 181P (2-4)
	Mar-Apr: 1611F (3-5)
	May-Jun: 9 (0-1)
	Jul-Aug: no runs
	Sep-Oct: P2 (0-2)
	Nov-Dec: 22332 (0-5)
Conclusion:	he has a good record in the spring — four of his five wins came during the period of 29 February to 7 April, the other in early January when 1-2 favourite for a Taunton bumper.

Summary of ideal conditions When racing on good to soft or faster going his record reads: 9P231162311F (4-12), improving to: 911611F (4-7) in the spring.

HELLO BUD (IRE)

11yo b g (N A Twiston-Davies)

Race type	NHF: 060 (0-3)
	Ptp: F3111 (3-5)
	Hdl: 97 (0-2)
	Chs: P004403111P116P11 (7-17)
Conclusion:	he's best over fences.
Fresh (absence	42 days or longer: 00FP47P1P1 (2-10)
since last race)	29-41 days: 0431 (1-4)
	28 days or less: 6931110011161 (7-13)
Conclusion:	most of his wins have come after a recent outing.

Summary of ideal conditions When racing over fences (including his Irish point-to-point form) his record reads: F3111P004403111P116P11 (10-22). His wins tend to come in groups of twos and threes and if we only consider his chase runs when returned to the track 28 days or sooner after a win his record improves to: 111111 (6-6).

HENNESSY (IRE)

8yo b g (Warren Greatrex)

Race type	NHF: 1279 (1-4)
	Hdl: F511424F0 (2-9)
	Chs: U21651 (2-6)
Conclusion:	he's effective over hurdles and fences.
Fresh (absence since last race)	140 days or longer: 1F111 (4-5)
	42-139 days: 20UF51 (1-6)
	28-41 days: 5 (0-1)
	27 days or less: 0242406 (0-7)
Conclusion:	he runs especially well when fresh – four of his five wins have come when rested for 20 weeks or longer.

Summary of ideal conditions When running fresh (after a break of six weeks or more) his record reads: 129F11UF151 (5-11), improving to: 1F111 (4-5) when rested for 20 weeks or longer.

I HAVE DREAMED (IRE)

7yo b g (G L Moore)

Race type	Hdl: 1224P62170 (2-10)
	Chs: 1 (1-1)
Conclusion:	he's a dual winner over hurdles and made a successful chase debut in a weak race at Huntingdon in April 2009.
Distance	2m-2m1f: 124621701 (3-9)
	2m1.5f-2m5f: 2P (0-2)
Conclusion:	he's best at 2m-2m1f.
Going	Good to firm or faster: 1 (1-1)
	Good: 1467 (1-4)
	Good to soft: 2210 (1-4)
	Soft/heavy: 2P (0-2)
Conclusion:	he seems to handle any conditions.
Track	Left-handed: P20 (0-3)
	Right-handed: 12246171 (3-8)
Conclusion:	he has yet to win left-handed but ran well at Cheltenham last season, finishing second of 17.
Fresh (absence since last race)	35 days or longer: 1P621 (2-5)
	34 days or less: 224701 (1-6)
Conclusion:	he runs well when fresh.

Summary of ideal conditions Although his chase win came after a break of just 26 days he might prove best when fresh – he scored first time out on the Flat for Terry Mills in 2005 and 2007 and has figures of: 1262 (1-4) in 2m contests for his current yard when rested for at least five weeks, with the first defeat by just two lengths when a 14-1 shot for a 17-runner handicap.

IMPERIAL COMMANDER (IRE)
8yo b g (N A Twiston-Davies)

Race type	NHF: 1 (1-1)
	Hdl: 46173 (1-5)
	Chs: 114161P (4-7)
Conclusion:	he's best over fences.
Distance	2m-2m2f: 1 (1-1)
	2m3f-2m5.5f: 4171111 (5-7)
	3m+: 6346P (0-5)
Conclusion:	he's best at about 2m4f.

Summary of ideal conditions Combine chase starts with racing from 2m3f-2m5.5f and his record becomes: 1111 (4-4).

I'MSINGINGTHEBLUES (IRE)
7yo b g (P F Nicholls)

Race type	NHF: 31 (1-2)
	Hdl: 113573 (2-6)
	Chs: 121182 (3-6)
Conclusion:	he's effective over hurdles and fences.
Distance	2m-2m2f: 3111357312118 (6-13)
	2m3f-2m5f: 2 (0-1)
Conclusion:	he struggled to see out the 2m4f trip when a nine-length second at Ayr on his final start last term.
Going	Good to firm or faster: no runs
	Good (good to firm in places): 1 (1-1)
	Good: 11132 (3-5)
	Good (good to soft places): 531 (1-3)
	Good to soft (good in places): 2 (0-1)
	Good to soft: 7 (0-1)
	Good to soft (soft in places): 318 (1-3)
	Soft/heavy: no runs
Conclusion:	he runs well on fast ground.

Fresh (absence First two runs each season or after a break of six weeks+:
since last race) 31115121 (5-8)
Other runs: 373182 (1-6)
Conclusion: he runs best when fresh.
Summary of ideal conditions When running fresh (first two runs each season or
when rested for six weeks or longer) at about 2m his record reads: 31115121 (5-8),
improving to: 1111 (4-4) on good or faster going.

JAUNTY FLIGHT

7yo b m (O Sherwood)

Race type	NHF: 0 (0-1)
	Hdl: U2442512114 (3-11)
	Chs: 1311 (3-4)
Conclusion:	she's effective over hurdles and fences.
Distance	2m-2m2f: 0U2423 (0-6)
	2m3f-2m6f: 511141 (4-6)
	3m+: 4211 (2-4)
Conclusion:	she struggled when dropped to 2m at Chepstow last season, finishing a 13-length third despite having the ground in her favour and going off as the 13-8 favourite.
Going	Good or faster: 044241 (1-6)
	Good to soft: 5 (0-1)
	Soft: 2111 (3-4)
	Heavy: U1231 (2-5)
Conclusion:	she's best on soft or heavy going.

Summary of ideal conditions Combine a distance of 2m3f or further with running
on soft or heavy going and her record becomes: 11111 (5-5).

JOE LIVELY (IRE)

10yo b g (C L Tizzard)

Race type	Hdl: 2110 (2-4)
	Chs: P112111564231615 (7-16)
Conclusion:	he's effective over hurdles and fences.
Going	Good to firm or faster: P201 (1-4)
	Good: 11121543 (4-8)
	Good to soft: 1625 (1-4)
	Soft: 116 (2-3)
	Heavy: 1 (1-1)
Conclusion:	the majority of his good-ground wins came at a low level and he seems much happier on soft or heavy going these days.

Field size	12 or more runners: P036 (0-4)
	8-11 runners: 211116411 (6-9)
	7 or fewer runners: 2111525 (3-7)

Conclusion: his prominent style of racing is best suited to small fields.

Summary of ideal conditions When racing in fields of 11 or fewer runners his record reads: 2111121115642115 (9-16), improving to: 111 (3-3) on soft or heavy going.

KALAHARI KING (FR)
8yo b g (Ferdy Murphy)

| **Race type** | Hdl: 3142431 (2-7) |
| | Chs: 1121212 (4-7) |

Conclusion: he has yet to finish out of the frame when racing over jumps.

| **Distance** | 2m-2m1f: 14243112212 (4-11) |
| | 2m4f: 311 (2-3) |

Conclusion: he is effective from 2m-2m4f and might stay further.

Going	Good or faster: 3431112 (3-7)
	Good to soft: 124121 (3-6)
	Soft/heavy: 2 (0-1)

Conclusion: he underperformed when tried on soft going at Haydock last season, finishing a 17-length second (10-11 favourite).

| **Track (chase** | Left-handed: 1221 (2-4) |
| **runs only)** | Right-handed: 112 (2-3) |

Conclusion: although twice a winner in low-grade right-handed chases he earned the comment 'jumped left' on occasions and made numerous errors when runner-up to Twist Magic at Sandown on his final start last term.

Summary of ideal conditions Combine hurdle or chase starts with running on good to soft or faster going and his record becomes: 3142431111212 (6-13), improving to: 111212 (4-6) over fences only, with the first defeat by a short head in the 2009 Arkle Chase.

KATIES TUITOR
6yo b g (C J Mann)

| **Race type** | Hdl: 211042321017140 (5-15) |

Conclusion: he has a good strike-rate over hurdles.

Field size	15 or more runners: 01011 (3-5)
	12-14 runners: 120 (1-3)
	11 or fewer runners: 2143274 (1-7)

Conclusion: he performs best in big fields.

Track	Left-handed: 22107 (1-5)
	Right-handed: 2110431140 (4-10)
Conclusion:	he won his sole start at left-handed Cheltenham but his other wins have come on right-handed tracks.
Headgear	Cheekpieces: 17140 (2-5)
Conclusion:	he has a good record when wearing cheekpieces.

Summary of ideal conditions When racing over hurdles in fields of 12 or more runners his record reads: 10210110 (4-8), improving to: 10110 (3-5) on right-handed tracks, with the latest defeat excusable as he reportedly needed the outing on his return from a nine-month break.

KEENAN'S FUTURE (IRE)

8yo ch g (Ian Williams)

Race type	NHF: 3 (0-1)
	Hdl: 11U4 (2-4)
	Chs: B3R15146613FP2193 (4-17)
Conclusion:	he won both his first two starts over hurdles and is a multiple chase winner.
Going	Good to firm or faster: no runs
	Good: 31546F43 (1-8)
	Good to soft: 1R111 (4-5)
	Soft: 3B63P2 (0-6)
	Heavy: 1U9 (1-3)
Conclusion:	he is likely to prove best on good to soft or softer going.
Track	Left-handed: 31U15146613P2143 (5-16)
	Right-handed: 1B3RF9 (1-6)
Conclusion:	the majority of his wins have come on left-handed tracks.
Field size	12 or more runners: 315463FP93 (1-10)
	11 or fewer runners: 1UB3R1161214 (5-12)
Conclusion:	he seems best in small fields, his chase wins coming in fields of eight, nine, eight and six runners.

Summary of ideal conditions When racing over hurdles, or on left-handed chase tracks, his record becomes: 11U15146613P2143 (6-16), improving to: 11U11613P21 (6-11) on ground slower than good.

KEEPITSECRET (IRE)

8yo b g (Jonjo O'Neill)

Race type	NHF: 14 (1-2)
	Hdl: 007115254U (2-10)
	Chs: P6116U0U7P12120F (4-16)
Conclusion:	he won twice over hurdles but has a better strike-rate over fences.
Distance	2m-2m2f: 14007P6 (1-7)
	2m3f-4.5f: 5U21 (1-4)
	2m5f-2m7f: 2546120 (1-7)
	3m+: 11U11U07PF (4-10)
Conclusion:	he's effective at 2m4f but is likely to prove best over longer trips.
Going	Good to firm or faster: 14124116110 (6-11)
	Good: 15U6U02F (1-8)
	Good to soft: 5U2 (0-3)
	Soft/heavy: 007P7P (0-6)
Conclusion:	the faster the going, the better he runs.
Time of year	Jan-Feb: 007PP (0-5)
	Mar-Apr: U (0-1)
	May-Jun: 11561121 (5-8)
	Jul-Aug: 120F (1-4)
	Sep-Oct: 14256U0 (1-7)
	Nov-Dec: 4U7 (0-3)
Conclusion:	he won a fast-ground bumper in October 2006 but his other wins have come in the spring or summer.

Summary of ideal conditions When racing over 2m3f or further in spring/summer (March-August), on good or faster going, his record reads: 11U111120F (6-10), with the runner-up effort by a shorthead when 20-1 for a Listed handicap chase at Market Rasen in July 2009.

KEMPSKI

9yo b g (R Nixon)

Race type	NHF: 5906 (0-4)
	Hdl: P22P00P5423634P5326113644P30781P4P1P1 (5-37)
	Chs: R6URP (0-5)
Conclusion:	he's best over hurdles.
Distance	2m-2m2f: 59062055376R4P (0-14)
	2m4f: P2P2634P113441P1P1 (5-18)
	2m5f+: P043R266P308UP (0-14)
Conclusion:	all his wins have come at 2m4f.

Going (hurdle starts only)	Good or faster: 03 (0-2)
	Good to soft: P22P (0-4)
	Soft: P0536P36407PP (0-13)
	Heavy: 2P4234536114P81411 (5-18)
Conclusion:	he has placed form on a variety of going but all his wins have come on a heavy surface.
Field size (hurdle starts only)	12 or more runners: 2P0036P2663078P4P1P (1-19)
	11 or fewer runners: P2P542345311344P11 (4-18)
Conclusion:	he's a front-runner and is better able to dominate when racing in small fields.
Course (hurdle starts only)	Ayr: P22523611P141P1 (5-15)
	Carlisle: P43P534 (0-7)
	Haydock: P (0-1)
	Kelso: P0266378P (0-9)
	Newcastle: 434 (0-3)
	Perth: 00 (0-2)
Conclusion:	he has yet to win away from Ayr.

Summary of ideal conditions When racing over hurdles at Ayr his record reads: P22523611P141P1 (5-15), improving to: 2211111 (5-7) at 2m4f on heavy going. From left-to-right: 2nd – placed at 50-1 in maiden company on only his second start over hurdles, 2nd – found only one too good when a blinkered first-time 14-1 shot in novice company, 1st (12-1), 1st (7-1), 1st (20-1), 1st (14-1) and 1st (9-2). All five wins came in handicap company, the majority after a recent outing.

KEW JUMPER (IRE)

10yo b g (Andrew Turnell)

Race type	Hdl: S9525 (0-5)
	Chs: 1722F1285326121533P41U (5-22)
Conclusion:	he's best over fences.
Going	Good or faster: 52517221851153341U (5-18)
	Good to soft or softer: S9F23262P (0-9)
Conclusion:	he's suited by fast going.
Time of year	Jan-Feb: 2F3P4 (0-5)
	Mar-Apr: 51212151U (4-9)
	May-Jun: 25 (0-2)
	Jul-Aug: no runs
	Sep-Oct: 173 (1-3)
	Nov-Dec: S9285263 (0-8)
Conclusion:	he tends to peak in the spring.

Summary of ideal conditions When racing over fences in March or April his record reads: 1212151U (4-8).

KNOWHERE (IRE)

11yo b g (N A Twiston-Davies)

Race type	Hdl: 11 (2-2)
	Chs: P11F22380U135P16UP180P (5-22)
Conclusion:	he's effective over hurdles and fences.
Distance	2m3f-2m5f110y: 11P11F22813P1 (6-13)
	3m-3m1f110y: 301 (1-3)
	3m2f+: U56UP80P (0-8)
Conclusion:	he won the 2008 Cotswold Chase over 3m1f110y at Cheltenham but that was a slowly run affair and he's likely to prove best over shorter trips.
Fresh (absence since last race)	First two runs or after a break of six weeks+: 11110131610 (7-11)
	Others: PF2238U5PUP8P (0-13)
Conclusion:	he runs especially well when fresh.
Class	Grade 1: 3060 (0-4)
	Grade 2: 1P211 (3-5)
	Grade 3: 528U35PUP8P (0-11)
	Others: 1111 (4-4)
Conclusion:	he might not be up to winning at Grade 1 level.

Summary of ideal conditions When running fresh (first two starts each season or after a break of six weeks or more) his record becomes: 11110131610 (7-11), improving to: 11111311 (7-8) when racing below Grade 1 level. His jumping still gives cause for concern, so he might prove best in small fields.

KORNATI KID

7yo b g (P J Hobbs)

Race type	NHF: 6 (0-1)
	Hdl: 34113 (2-5)
	Chs: 24116 (2-5)
Conclusion:	he's effective over hurdles and fences.
Distance	2m-2m2f: 6 (0-1)
	2m3f-2m7f: 3411 (2-4)
	3m-3m1f: 32411 (2-5)
	3m2f+: 6 (0-1)
Conclusion:	he's likely to prove best at about 3m.
Going	Good or faster: 64 (0-2)
	Good to soft: 34126 (1-5)
	Soft/heavy: 1311 (3-4)
Conclusion:	he has a good strike-rate on soft or heavy going.

Track	Left-handed: 64416 (1-5)
	Right-handed: 311321 (3-6)
Conclusion:	he won at left-handed Wetherby last term but only scraped home by a neck after jumping persistently out to his right and is likely to prove best on right-handed tracks.

Summary of ideal conditions When racing right-handed his record reads: 311321 (3-6).

LASKARI (FR)

10yo b g (P R Webber)

Race type	Hdl: 947 (0-3)
	Chs: 13514P32P32P1125P2P (4-19)
Conclusion:	he's best over fences.
Distance	(chase starts only)
	2m-2m2.5f: 5 (0-1)
	2m3f-2m5.5f: 131432P32112 (4-12)
	2m6f+: PP25PP (0-6)
Conclusion:	he's best at about 2m4f.
Field size	12 or more runners: 32P25PP (0-7)
(chase runs only)	11 or fewer runners: 13514PP32112 (4-12)
Conclusion:	he has yet to win in a big field but did finish second of 18 at Kempton last season.
Fresh	First two runs each season or after a break of about five weeks+:
	94711P332P112 (4-13)
	Other runs: 3542P25PP (0-9)
Conclusion:	he runs well when fresh.

Summary of ideal conditions Combine chase starts with racing from 2m3f-2m5.5f and his record becomes: 131432P32112 (4-12), improving to: 11332112 (4-8) when fresh (first two runs each season or when rested for approximately five weeks). The majority of his wins have come right-handed on good to soft or faster going.

L'AVENTURE (FR)

10yo b m (Nick Williams)

Race type	Hdl: 1066 (1-4)
	Chs: 2F112422124644041537782P40873832F5367 (4-37)
Conclusion:	she landed one of her four starts over hurdles but is better known as a chaser.
Going	Good to firm or faster: 220 (0-3)
	Good: F1420478367 (1-11)
	Good to soft: 140163832F (2-10)
	Soft: 12126467P47 (2-11)
	Heavy: 453825 (0-6)
Conclusion:	she's best on good to soft or softer going.
Field size	12 or more runners: 4640415376782P4073832F567 (1-25)
	10-11 runners: 202483 (0-6)
	8-9 runners: 16 (1-2)
	7 or fewer runners: 2F112421 (3-8)
Conclusion:	she likes to race prominently but tends to lose her position when racing in big fields before staying on again in the closing stages.

Summary of ideal conditions Combine hurdle or chase starts with running on good to soft or softer going, in fields of nine or fewer runners, and her record becomes: 1211 (3-4). She has yet to win for current trainer Nick Williams but went close in the London National at Sandown (December 2008) and wasn't beaten far when third of 10 on unsuitably fast going at Hereford (March 2009).

LE BURF (FR)

8yo b g (G R I Smyly)

Race type	NHF: 6P20 (0-4)
	Hdl: 46120005 (1-8)
	Chs: 3F2321511F5 (3-11)
Conclusion:	he's best over fences.
Distance	2m-2m2f: 6P2012003F23250 (1-15)
	2m3f-2m5f: 461511F5 (3-8)
Conclusion:	he's effective at 2m but best over further.
Going	Good or faster: 6P00015 (1-7)
	Good to soft: 2463F215F (1-9)
	Soft/heavy: 1202351 (2-7)
Conclusion:	he has a superior strike-rate on soft/heavy going.

Track	Left-handed: 6204600F2305F5 (0-14)
	Right-handed: P12321511 (4-9)
Conclusion:	he has yet to win on a left-handed track.

Summary of ideal conditions When racing right-handed his record over obstacles reads: 12321511 (4-8). These figures improve to: 12111 (4-5) when only considering his runs at 2m3f or further (or at shorter trips on soft/heavy going).

LIGHTNING STRIKE (GER)

6yo ch g (Miss Venetia Williams)

Race type	Hdl: 29511P367 (2-9)
	Chs: 1131P (3-5)
Conclusion:	he's effective over hurdles and fences.
Field size	12 or more runners: 956P (0-4)
	10-11 runners: 3 (0-1)
	8-9 runners: 2P7 (0-3)
	7 or fewer runners: 111131 (5-6)
Conclusion:	all his wins have come in small fields.

Summary of ideal conditions When racing in fields of seven or fewer runners his record reads: 111131 (5-6), with the sole defeat coming over fences at Kempton where he made several jumping errors before keeping on late. He has winning form from 2m-3m and on ground ranging from good through to heavy.

LODGE LANE (IRE)

8yo b g (V R A Dartnall)

Race type	NHF: 110 (2-3)
	Hdl: 1101 (3-4)
	Chs: 1PP2F2 (1-6)
Conclusion:	he has a 75% strike-rate over hurdles and made a winning start to his chase career.
Distance	2m-2m2f: 110 (2-3)
	2m3f-2m5f: 11 (2-2)
	3m+: 011PP2F2 (2-8)
Conclusion:	he is effective over a variety of trips.
Going	Good to firm or faster: no runs
	Good: 12F2 (1-4)
	Good to soft: 001P (1-4)
	Soft: 11P (2-3)
	Heavy: 11 (2-2)
Conclusion:	he has an especially good record on soft or heavy going.

Course	Cheltenham: 00FP (0-4)
	Exeter: 11 (2-2)
	Fontwell: 1 (1-1)
	Kempton: P (0-1)
	Lingfield: 2 (0-1)
	Perth: 12 (1-2)
	Uttoxeter: 11 (2-2)
Conclusion:	he has a poor record at Cheltenham.
Headgear	Blinkers: 2F2 (0-3)
Conclusion:	his jumping, which already lacked fluency, was not helped by the addition of blinkers for his final three starts last season.

Summary of ideal conditions When racing at tracks other than Cheltenham his record reads: 111111P22 (6-9), improving to: 111111P (6-7) without headgear.

MADISON DU BERLAIS (FR)
8yo b g (D E Pipe)

Distance	2m-2m2f: 31113381153 (5-11)
	2m3f-2m5f: U64173 (1-6)
	3m+: 4425F61181 (3-10)
Conclusion:	his last three wins have come over 3m or further but he is effective at shorter trips, especially when the ground is soft or heavy.
Going	Good or faster: 1133342F61 (3-10)
	Good to soft: 3575118 (2-7)
	Soft/heavy: U186411314 (4-10)
Conclusion:	he handles most conditions.
Fresh (absence since last race)	29 days or longer: U38245F618 (1-10)
	28 days or less: 31113641153172411 (8-17)
Conclusion:	the majority of his wins have come after a recent outing.
Track	Flat: U31131131424F111 (8-16)
	Significant undulations: 18645573568 (1-11)
Conclusion:	he has a superior strike-rate on flat tracks – his last six wins coming at Aintree, Kempton, Newbury (twice), Southwell and Warwick.
Field size	16 or more runners: 374F8 (0-5)
	12-15 runners: 645261 (1-6)
	11 or fewer runners: U311138113134511 (8-16)
Conclusion:	he landed the 2008 Hennessy in a field of 15 but his other wins have come against 10 or fewer rivals.

Headgear Cheekpieces: 1181 (3-4)
Conclusion: he has a good record in cheekpieces.
Summary of ideal conditions When racing on flat tracks his record reads:
U31131131424F111 (8-16), improving to: 111 (3-3) in cheekpieces, with all three
wins coming over 3m or further.

MALJIMAR (IRE)

9yo b g (Nick Williams)

Race type	NHF: 2 (0-1)
	Hdl: 6P14 (1-4)
	Chs: F23132U41U72P (2-13)
Conclusion:	he's best over fences.
Distance	2m-2m1f: 264 (0-3)
	2m2f-2m5f: P1423132U1U7 (3-12)
	3m+: F27 (0-3)
Conclusion:	his wins have come at about 2m4f but he stays further.
Going	Good to firm or faster: 14 (1-2)
	Good: 6P24 (0-4)
	Good to soft: 2F231U27 (1-8)
	Soft: 31U7 (1-4)
	Heavy: no runs
Conclusion:	his best recent efforts have come on good to soft or soft going.
Fresh (absence	42 days or longer: 26P1F12U172 (3-11)
since last race)	28-41 days: 3U (0-2)
	27 days or less: 4234P (0-5)
Conclusion:	he runs especially well when fresh.

Summary of ideal conditions When running fresh (after a break of six weeks or
longer) his record becomes: 26P1F12U172 (3-11), improving to: F12U172 (2-7) for
current trainer Nick Williams. From left to right: F – tipped up four out at Chepstow
when still travelling well (3m, good to soft), 1st – landed a soft-ground 2m3f
handicap chase at Newbury, 2nd – beaten by a neck in a valuable 19-runner
handicap chase at Cheltenham, U – unseated rider at the first fence, 1st, 7th –
"outpaced" though not disgraced in the 2008 Paddy Power Gold Cup, and 2nd –
beaten by a neck at the Cheltenham festival (3m, good to soft). He'll be aimed at the
2010 Grand National and, given that the progeny of his sire Un Desperado do best
at the age of 10, he should be at his physical peak for Aintree.

MON MOME (FR)

9yo b g (Miss Venetia Williams)

Race type	Hdl: 7U3624532 (0-9)
	Chs: U2121121U422434P609218781 (6-25)
Conclusion:	he's best over fences.
Going	Good to firm or faster: no runs
	Good: 45U22U09 (0-8)
	Good to soft: 7214P36211 (3-10)
	Soft/heavy: U361211422438278 (3-16)
Conclusion:	he seems best suited by good to soft or softer going.
Fresh	Seasonal debuts: 7U4P2 (0-5)
Conclusion:	he has yet to win at the first time of asking.
Class (chase	1: U22434P60918781 (2-15)
runs only)	2: 2142 (1-4)
	3: U2211 (2-5)
	4: 1 (1-1)
Conclusion:	he improved last season, recording his first Class 1 victory (at Cheltenham in December 2008) before causing a 100-1 shock in the Grand National.

Summary of ideal conditions When racing over fences on good to soft or softer going, excluding seasonal debuts, his record is: 121112243460918781 (6-18).

MOON OVER MIAMI (GER)

8yo b g (C J Mann)

Race type	Hdl: 48112212 (3-8)
	Chs: 5141P66424520 (2-13)
Conclusion:	he's effective over hurdles and fences.
Distance	2m-2m2.5f: 481122125141P664220 (5-19)
	2m3f-2m5f: 45 (0-2)
Conclusion:	he's best at about 2m.
Going	Good or faster: 112212560 (3-9)
	Good to soft: 48P652 (0-6)
	Soft/heavy: 141424 (2-6)
Conclusion:	his best recent efforts have come on slow going.
Track	Left-handed: 481111P6642420 (4-14)
	Right-handed: 1222545 (1-7)
Conclusion:	four of his five wins have come on left-handed tracks – at Cheltenham (twice), Uttoxeter and Newbury.

Fresh (absence 42 days or longer: 425P6 (0-5)
since last race) 29-41 days: 2622 (0-4)
28 days or less: 811211414450 (5-12)
Conclusion: all his wins came when returned to the track 28 days or less after his previous outing.
Summary of ideal conditions When racing left-handed at 2m-2m2.5f, after a recent run (28 days or less), his record becomes: 8111140 (4-7), with the two most recent defeats coming in cheekpieces (he has yet to win when wearing headgear).

MORGAN BE
9yo b g (Mrs K Walton)
Race type NHF: 700 (0-3)
Hdl: P934211 (2-7)
Chs: 5211682412 (3-10)
Conclusion: he's effective over hurdles and fences.
Going Good or faster: 0P8 (0-3)
Good to soft: 02 (0-2)
Soft: 9342164 (1-7)
Heavy: 71521112 (4-8)
Conclusion: the softer the going, the better he runs.
Race conditions Handicap: 11682412 (3-8)
Non-handicap: 700P93421521 (2-12)
Conclusion: he has a superior strike-rate in handicap company.
Course Ayr: 211111 (5-6)
Others: 700P9345268242 (0-14)
Conclusion: he was only just denied in the 2009 Eider chase at Newcastle but has still to win away from Ayr.
Summary of ideal conditions When racing over obstacles on good to soft or softer going his record reads: 934211521162412 (5-15), improving to: 211111 (5-6) at Ayr only.

MR BIG (IRE)
8yo ch g (C J Mann)

Race type	Hdl: 0 (0-1)
	Chs: 1P2211322132 (4-12)
Conclusion:	he's best over fences.
Going	Good to firm or faster: 12 (1-2)
	Good: 212213 (2-6)
	Good to soft: P (0-1)
	Soft: 23 (0-2)
	Heavy: 01 (1-2)
Conclusion:	his heavy-ground win came in a weak contest and he's likely to prove best on good or faster going.
Field size	16 or more runners: 22 (0-2)
(chase runs	12-15 runners: P211 (2-4)
only)	10-11 runners: 132 (1-3)
	9 or fewer runners: 132 (1-3)
Conclusion:	he won a four-runner Hunters' Chase in Ireland but his two small-field runs for Charlie Mann resulted in heavy defeats (by 22 and 38 lengths) and it looks as though he prefers a big field/strong pace.
Headgear	Cheekpieces: 12211322132 (4-11)
	Without headgear: 0P (0-2)
Conclusion:	he has yet to finish outside of the first three when wearing cheekpieces.

Summary of ideal conditions When running in cheekpieces his record reads: 12211322132 (4-11), improving to: 2121 (2-4) when racing on good or faster going in fields of 12 or more runners. His wins came over distances of 2m5f-3m.

MY PETRA
6yo b m (N J Henderson)

Race type	Hdl: 111406381 (4-9)
	Chs: 3122P12FP (2-9)
Conclusion:	she's effective over hurdles and fences.
Distance	Good to firm or faster: 131 (2-3)
	Good: 162P1 (2-5)
	Good to soft: 14031282FP (2-10)
	Soft/heavy: no runs
Conclusion:	she seems happiest on fast ground.
Track	Left-handed: 110632P1FP (3-10)
	Right-handed: 14312812 (3-8)
Conclusion:	she's effective both left-handed and right-handed.

Field size	12 or more runners: 2PFP (0-4)
(chase runs	8-11 runners: no runs
only)	7 or fewer runners: 31212 (2-5)
Conclusion:	both her chase wins came in small fields.
Fresh	First two runs each season or after a break of at least five weeks: 1103111P (5-8)
	Other runs: 146322P82F (1-10)
Conclusion:	she runs well when fresh.

Summary of ideal conditions Aside from her big-field (12 or more runners) chase outings, her record reads: 1114063312112 (6-13), improving to: 1103111 (5-7) when fresh (first two runs each season or after a break of five weeks or more). The 'duck egg' came when 50-1 for the 2007 Triumph Hurdle and the third place came on her chase debut when pitched straight into Grade 2 company at Kempton. She has winning form from 2m-2m3f though does stay further.

MYLORD COLLONGES (FR)

9yo bl g (M G Rimell)

Race type	Hdl: 8700 (0-4)
	Chs: 7F4P4112131254 (4-14)
Conclusion:	he's best over fences.
Distance	2m-2m2f: 015 (1-3)
	2m3f-2m5f: 707P1121324 (3-11)
	2m6f+: 8F44 (0-4)
Conclusion:	he's best at about 2m4f.
Going	Good or faster: 00P24 (0-5)
	Good to soft: F411325 (2-7)
	Soft/heavy: 877411 (2-6)
Conclusion:	he's best on good to soft or slower going.
Headgear	Cheekpieces: 4112131254 (4-10)
	Without headgear: 87007F4P (0-8)
Conclusion:	he improved for the fitting of cheekpieces.

Summary of ideal conditions Combine chase starts of 2m-2m5f with racing on good to soft or softer going, when wearing cheekpieces, and his record becomes: 1113125 (4-7).

NACARAT (FR)

8yo gr g (T R George)

Race type	Hdl: P (0-1)
	Chs: 1P2F2113 (3-8)
Conclusion:	he ran a disappointing race at Cheltenham in April 2008 when he tried over hurdles.
Distance	2m-2m2.5f: 2 (0-1)
	2m3f-2m5.5f: 1P2FP13 (2-7)
	3m+: 1 (1-1)
Conclusion:	he was very impressive when stepped up to 3m for the Racing Post Chase at Kempton in February 2009.
Going	Good to firm or faster: no runs
	Good: 13 (1-2)
	Good to soft: P2FP (0-4)
	Soft: 121 (2-3)
	Heavy: no runs
Conclusion:	he has a good record on soft ground.
Track	Left-handed: P2FP13 (1-6)
	Right-handed: 121 (2-3)
Conclusion:	he has a superior strike-rate on right-handed tracks but did win at left-handed Doncaster last season.
Track	Flat: 12F113 (3-6)
	Significant undulations: PP2 (0-3)
Conclusion:	all his wins have come on flat courses (Doncaster, Kempton and Wincanton) and he has pulled-up in both starts at Cheltenham.
Fresh (absence since last race)	42 days or longer: 12 (1-2)
	28-41 days: 2F113 (2-5)
	27 days or less: PP (0-2)
Conclusion:	he runs well when fresh.

Summary of ideal conditions When racing on flat tracks his record reads: 12F113 (3-6), improving to: 11 (2-2) on soft going.

NATIVE CORAL (IRE)
11yo ch g (N G Richards)

Race type	Hdl: 1P1 (2-3)
	Chs: 12163414F231P (4-13)
Conclusion:	he's effective over hurdles and fences.
Going	Good to firm or faster: 21 (1-2)
	Good: 1434F21P (2-8)
	Good to soft: 11 (2-2)
	Soft/heavy: 1P43 (1-4)
Conclusion:	he's suited by good to soft or faster going.
Course	Ascot: 4 (0-1)
	Ayr: 14 (1-2)
	Bangor: F (0-1)
	Carlisle: P (0-1)
	Doncaster: 3 (0-1)
	Haydock: 2 (0-1)
	Kelso: 3 (0-1)
	Market Rasen: 6P (0-2)
	Musselburgh: 1 (1-1)
	Perth: 1211 (3-4)
	Stratford: 1 (1-1)
Conclusion:	he's suited by flat/sharp tracks (e.g. Musselburgh and Perth).
Fresh (absence	35 days or longer: 11213411F31P (6-12)
since last race)	34 days or less: P642 (0-4)
Conclusion:	all his wins came when fresh (after breaks of 286, 88, 62, 58, 47 and 44 days).

Summary of ideal conditions When running fresh (after a break of at least five weeks) his record reads: 11213411F31P (6-12), improving to: 12111 (4-5) at Musselburgh or Perth only.

NEMETAN (FR)

8yo ch g (R H & Mrs S Alner)

Race type	Hdl: 998P52127F5 (1-11)
	Chs: F13346122113U2 (4-14)
Conclusion:	he's effective over hurdles but has a superior strike-rate over fences.
Course	Chepstow: 6225 (0-4)
	Exeter: 51211F (3-6)
	Folkestone: 3 (0-1)
	Hereford: 4 (0-1)
	Kempton: 13U (1-3)
	Leicester: 99 (0-2)
	Newton Abbot: 22 (0-2)
	Plumpton: P (0-1)
	Taunton: F13 (1-3)
	Towcester: 7 (0-1)
	Warwick: 8 (0-1)
Conclusion:	all his wins have come on right-handed tracks and he has an especially good record at Exeter.
Fresh	Seasonal debuts: 9567 (0-4)
Conclusion:	he is likely to need his first run of the season.

Summary of ideal conditions When racing right-handed, excluding seasonal debuts, his record reads: 9F133412111F3U (5-14), improving to: 1211F (3-5) at Exeter only. He's effective over a variety of trips and ground but probably needs at least 2m3f if conditions are on the fast side.

NENUPHAR COLLONGES (FR)

8yo b g (A King)

Race type	Hdl: 21214 (2-5)
	Chs: 11F2117634 (4-10)
Conclusion:	he's effective over hurdles and fences.
Distance	2m-2m7.5f: 11F222 (2-6)
	3m+: 111417634 (4-9)
Conclusion:	he improved for the step up to 3m+.
Going	Good to firm or faster: no runs
	Good: 14 (1-2)
	Good to soft: 1F13 (2-4)
	Soft: 1212174 (3-7)
	Heavy: 26 (0-2)
Conclusion:	he seems best on good to soft or softer going.

Track	Aintree: 4 (0-1)
	Bangor: 11 (2-2)
	Cheltenham: 2113 (2-4)
	Chepstow: 7 (0-1)
	Exeter: F (0-1)
	Haydock: 6 (0-1)
	Hereford: 1 (1-1)
	Leicester: 2 (0-1)
	Punchestown: 4 (0-1)
	Uttoxeter: 1 (1-1)
	Warwick: 2 (0-1)
Conclusion:	he takes an age to hit top gear in his races and is clearly happiest on stiff/galloping tracks such as Cheltenham.
Field size (chase runs only)	12 or more runners: 7634 (0-4)
	11 or fewer runners: 11F211 (4-6)
Conclusion:	he has yet to win over fences in a big field.

Summary of ideal conditions Since joining his current trainer Alan King his record in Britain and Ireland, at 3m or further, stands at: 111417634 (4-9), improving to: 11141 (4-5) if we knock out his chase runs in fields of 12 or more runners.

NEPTUNE COLLONGES (FR)

8yo gr g (P F Nicholls)

Race type	Hdl: 14121136 (4-8)
	Ch: 1111U121F813131F14 (10-18)
Conclusion:	he's effective over hurdles and fences.
Field size	12 or more runners: 14834 (1-5)
	8-11 runners: 11U123216F131F (6-14)
	7 or fewer runners: 1111111 (7-7)
Conclusion:	he still takes the occasional liberty with his fences and is likely to prove best in small fields.

Summary of ideal conditions When racing in small fields (11 or fewer runners) his record is: 11U1112113216F13111F1 (13-21), including a seven-from-seven haul in fields of seven or fewer runners.

NICTO DE BEAUCHENE (FR)

8yo b g (R H & Mrs S Alner)

Race type	Hdl: 8950 (0-4)
	Chs: 3FF21531 (2-8)
Conclusion:	he's best over fences.
Going	Good or faster: 0F (0-2)
	Good to soft: 8F13 (1-4)
	Soft: 93251 (1-5)
	Heavy: 5 (0-1)
Conclusion:	he seems happiest on good to soft or softer going.
Field size	12 or more runners: FF (0-2)
(chase starts	11 or fewer runners: 321531 (2-6)
only)	
Conclusion:	he tends to make at least one serious jumping error per race and is likely to prove best in small fields.

Summary of ideal conditions Combine chase starts with racing in fields of 11 or fewer runners and his record becomes: 321531 (2-6), with the fifth place coming over Wincanton's tricky fences.

NOSTRINGSATTACHED (IRE)

8yo b g (Jonjo O'Neill)

Race type	Hdl: 6706324571326 (1-13)
	Chs: U422112 (2-7)
Conclusion:	he's best over fences.
Distance	2m-2m3f: 370U (0-4)
	2m5f-2m6.5f: 64532211 (2-8)
	3m+: 32741262 (1-8)
Conclusion:	he needs a trip of at least 2m4f.
Going	Good to firm or faster: U671322 (1-7)
	Good: 6324526112 (2-10)
	Good to soft: 4 (0-1)
	Soft/heavy: 70 (0-2)
Conclusion:	he prefers fast ground.
Headgear	Cheekpieces: 74132622112 (3-11)
	Without headgear: 670U63245 (0-9)
Conclusion:	all his wins have come when wearing cheekpieces.

Summary of ideal conditions Combine a distance of 2m4f or further with racing on good or faster going, when wearing cheekpieces, and his record becomes: 7132622112 (3-10), improving to: 22112 (2-5) over fences only.

NOTRE PERE (FR)
8yo b g (J T R Dreaper)

Race type	NHF: 2221 (1-4)
	Hdl: 133 (1-3)
	Chs: 211F63P41121 (5-12)
Conclusion:	he's best over fences.
Distance	2m-2m2f: 2221 (1-4)
	2m3f-2m6.5f: 1332164 (2-7)
	3m-3m2f: 1F121 (3-5)
	3m4f+: 3P1 (1-3)
Conclusion:	he's a thorough stayer.
Going	Good or faster: P (0-1)
	Good to yielding: 13 (1-2)
	Yielding: no runs
	Yielding to soft: 6 (0-1)
	Soft: 22F412 (1-6)
	Soft to heavy: 21 (1-2)
	Heavy: 2113311 (4-7)
Conclusion:	the softer the going, the better he runs.
Fresh	Seasonal debuts: 2224 (0-4)
Conclusion:	he has yet to win at the first time of asking.

Summary of ideal conditions Combine chase starts with racing over 3m or further and his record becomes: 1F3P1121 (4-8), improving to: F1121 (3-5) on soft or heavy going.

OAKFIELD LEGEND
8yo b g (P S Payne)

Race type	NHF: 50 (0-2)
	Hdl: P67P45 (0-6)
	Chs: 1P6472F12F323213 (3-16)
Conclusion:	he's best over fences.
Distance	2m-2m5.5f: P473 (0-4)
(chase runs	2m6f-2m7.5f: 16213 (2-5)
only)	3m+: F2F2213 (1-7)
Conclusion:	he needs a trip of at least 2m6f.

Going (chase runs only)	Good to firm or faster: P1 (1-2)
	Good: 1647F3321 (2-9)
	Good to soft: 2F23 (0-4)
	Soft/heavy: 2 (0-1)
Conclusion:	he needs fast ground.

Summary of ideal conditions Combine chase starts of 2m6f or further with running on good or faster going and his record becomes: 161F321 (3-7).

OFFICIER DE RESERVE (FR)
7yo br g (P F Nicholls)

Race type	Hdl: 3419 (1-4)
	Chs: F1112164C4P (4-11)
Conclusion:	he ran a disappointing race when returned to hurdles at Hereford last season and is likely to prove best over fences.
Field size	12 or more runners: 36PC49P (0-7)
	11 or fewer runners: F1112411 (5-8)
Conclusion:	he tends to make jumping errors when asked to race in big fields.

Summary of ideal conditions When racing in fields of 11 or fewer runners his record reads: F1112411 (5-8). A trip of 3m+ on good to soft or softer going is ideal.

OH CRICK (FR)
6yo ch g (A King)

Race type	Hdl: 6211119 (4-7)
	Chs: 1423F211 (3-8)
Conclusion:	he has a good strike-rate over hurdles and fences.
Distance	2m-2m1f: 111194211 (6-9)
	2m1.5f-2m5f: 6213F2 (1-6)
Conclusion:	he's best at about 2m.
Fresh	Seasonal debuts: 64 (0-2)
Conclusion:	he will probably need his first run of the season.
Field size	16 or more runners: 119 (2-3)
	12-15 runners: 611 (2-3)
	10-11 runners: 214 (1-3)
	9 or fewer runners: 1123F2 (2-6)
Conclusion:	he's suited by coming late off a strong pace and is likely to prove best in big fields.

Summary of ideal conditions When racing at 2m-2m1f his record reads: 111194211 (6-9), with the latest defeat by a head. His 2m-2m1f figures improve to: 11911 (4-5) if we only consider his runs in fields of 12 or more runners. His last six wins have come on good to soft or faster going.

OISEAU DE NUIT (FR)

7yo b g (P J Hobbs)

Race type	NHF: 0 (0-1)
	Hdl: P59202F244 (0-10)
	Chs: 11U31271 (4-8)
Conclusion:	he's best over fences.
Track	Left-handed: 00F11 (2-5)
	Right-handed: P592211U327244 (2-14)
Conclusion:	the majority of his runs have taken place on right-handed tracks but he has a 40% strike-rate when racing left-handed.
Course (chase runs only)	Cheltenham: 1 (1-1)
	Huntingdon: 11 (2-2)
	Lingfield: 1 (1-1)
	Ludlow: 7 (0-1)
	Wincanton: U32 (0-3)
Conclusion:	there's room for improvement where his jumping is concerned and he tends to get found out by the tricky fences at Wincanton.

Summary of ideal conditions When racing over fences away from Wincanton his record reads: 11171 (4-5), with the sole defeat at Ludlow where he earned the comment 'blundered badly 3 out, not recover' from the *Racing Post*. All these runs took place at about 2m with the wins coming on ground ranging from good to soft through to heavy.

OLD BENNY

8yo b g (A King)

Race type	NHF: 227 (0-3)
	Hdl: 5221127 (2-7)
	Chs: 32214 (1-5)
Conclusion:	he's effective over hurdles and fences.
Distance	1m5f-2m7f: 4275 (0-4)
	3m+: 22112732214 (3-11)
Conclusion:	he needs a trip of at least 3m and he stays marathon distances well – his latest win came in the 4m National Hunt Chase Challenge Cup at the 2008 Cheltenham Festival.
Going	Good or faster: 4224 (0-4)
	Good to soft: 5721 (1-4)
	Soft/heavy: 2721132 (2-7)
Conclusion:	he's effective on good ground but all his wins have come on good to soft or softer going.

Summary of ideal conditions When racing over 3m or further his record is: 22112732214 (3-11), with the sole unplaced effort coming in a Pertemps qualifier (the fourth place came in a 24-runner handicap chase). On good to soft or softer going only his record over 3m or further improves to: 21173221 (3-8). He missed the 2008/2009 season but is expected to return to action in November before a tilt at the Welsh National the following month.

OLIVINO (GER)
8yo ch g (B J Llewellyn)

Race conditions	Non-handicap hurdle: 574221 (1-6)
	Handicap hurdle: P8512115 (3-8)
Conclusion:	he won a weak maiden when 4-9 favourite but his other wins have come in handicap company.
Distance	2m-2m1.5f: 74221P5111 (4-10)
	2m2f-2m5f: 5825 (0-4)
Conclusion:	he's best at about 2m.
Going	Good to firm or faster: 572151 (2-6)
	Good: 42211 (2-5)
	Good to soft: 85 (0-2)
	Soft/heavy: P (0-1)
Conclusion:	he needs good or faster going.
Course	Chepstow: 8 (0-1)
	Exeter: 5 (0-1)
	Fakenham: 2 (0-1)
	Fontwell: 5 (0-1)
	Hereford: 7 (0-1)
	Newton Abbot: 21115 (3-5)
	Towcester: P (0-1)
	Wetherby: 1 (1-1)
	Worcester: 42 (0-2)
Conclusion:	he runs on well on sharp left-handed tracks, especially at Newton Abbot.

Summary of ideal conditions When racing over hurdles from 2m-2m1.5f his record reads: 74221P5111 (4-10), improving to: 4221111 (4-7) on good or faster going and on left-handed tracks.

OSCAR BAY (IRE)
7yo b/br g (J D Frost)

Race type	Hdl: 3342101 (2-7)
	Chs: 1242313FP (2-9)
Conclusion:	he's effective over hurdles and fences.
Distance	2m-2m1.5f: 332 (0-3)
	2m2f-2m4.5f: 4210112313 (4-10)
	2m5f-2m7.5f: P (0-1)
	3m+: 4F (0-2)
Conclusion:	he seems best at about 2m4f.
Going	Good to firm or faster: 3P (0-2)
	Good: 01113F (3-6)
	Good to soft: 12 (1-2)
	Soft: 3423 (0-4)
	Heavy: 24 (0-2)
Conclusion:	he handles most conditions but his wins have come on good or good to soft going.
Track	Left-handed: 32111FP (3-7)
	Right-handed: 341024233 (1-9)
Conclusion:	he earned comments like 'hung left' and 'hung left throughout' when beaten four times at right-handed Exeter last season and is happiest on left-handed tracks.
Fresh	Seasonal debuts: 325 (0-3)
Conclusion:	he usually needs his first run of the season.

Summary of ideal conditions Aside from seasonal debuts, his record left-handed reads: 2111F (3-5), improving to: 2111 (3-4) over trips short of 3m, with the sole defeat by two lengths when 20-1 for a 16-runner novices' hurdle on heavy ground.

OUT THE BLACK (IRE)
11yo b/br g (P J Hobbs)

Race type	Hdl: P (0-1)
Chs: 131F4S34414U15254123 (5-20)	
Conclusion:	he's best over fences.
Going	Good or faster: 131F4S41P4U1525123 (5-18)
	Good to soft: 4 (0-1)
	Soft/heavy: 34 (0-2)
Conclusion:	he prefers fast going.
Fresh (absence	35 days or longer: 1S4P415541 (3-10)
since last race)	28-34 days: 12 (1-2)
	27 days or less: 31F434U23 (1-9)
Conclusion:	he runs well when fresh.

Summary of ideal conditions When racing over fences on good or faster going his record reads: 131F4S414U1525123 (5-17), improving to: 1S41P415251 (4-11) when rested for 28 days or longer.

PABLO DU CHARMIL (FR)
8yo ch g (D E Pipe)

Race type	Hdl: 22U00 (0-5)
	Chs: 111016358136064 (5-15)
Conclusion:	he won over hurdles in France but his UK wins have come over fences.
Going	Good to firm or faster: 1 (1-1)
	Good: 0163836 (1-7)
	Good to soft: 2U105004 (1-8)
	Soft: 1 (1-1)
	Heavy: 216 (1-3)
Conclusion:	he seems effective on any going.
Field size	12 or more runners: 2U000604 (0-8)
	10-11 runners: 638 (0-3)
	8-9 runners: 6 (0-1)
	6-7 runners: 2513 (1-4)
	5 or fewer runners: 1111 (4-4)
Conclusion:	his jumping remains far from fluent and all his wins have come in very small fields.
Fresh	Seasonal debuts: 2111 (3-4)
Conclusion:	he has a fine record first-time out.

Summary of ideal conditions When racing over fences in fields of 11 or fewer runners his record reads: 11116358136 (5-11), improving to: 111 (3-3) on his seasonal debuts only.

PACCO (FR)
6yo b g (O Sherwood)

Race type	NHF: 64 (0-2)
	Hdl: 79511 (2-5)
	Chs: 413713P (2-7)
Conclusion:	he has winning form over hurdles and fences.
Distance	2m-2m5.5f: 64751141313P (4-12)
	2m6f+: 97 (0-2)
Conclusion:	all his wins came over trips short of 2m6f.
Fresh	Seasonal debuts: 64 (0-2)
Conclusion:	he might need his first run of the season.

Race conditions Handicap: 11413713P (4-9)

Non-handicap: 64795 (0-5)

Conclusion: all his wins came in handicap company.

Summary of ideal conditions When racing in handicap company his record reads: 11413713P (4-9), improving to: 111313P (4-7) if we ignore his seasonal debuts and runs over 2m6f or further. The latest defeat came after a two-month break when he was probably in need of the outing.

PAGAN STARPRINCESS
5yo b m (G M Moore)

Race type	Hdl: 1222F52P113P (3-12)
Conclusion:	she has a 25% strike-rate over hurdles.
Distance	2m-2m2.5f: 1222F5113 (3-9)
	2m3f-2m5f: P (0-1)
	2m6f+: 2P (0-2)
Conclusion:	all her wins have come at about 2m but her runner-up effort over 2m6.5f at Kelso in October 2008 suggests that she'll be capable of scoring over further this term.
Going	Good to firm or faster: no runs
	Good: F2 (0-2)
	Good to soft: 2225P (0-5)
	Soft/heavy: 1P113 (3-5)
Conclusion:	all her wins have come on soft going.
Fresh (absence since last race)	42 days or longer: 1221 (2-4)
	35-41 days: 21 (1-2)
	28-34 days: F (0-1)
	27 days or less: 25P3P (0-5)
Conclusion:	she's best when fresh.

Summary of ideal conditions When rested for five weeks or longer her record reads: 122211 (3-6), improving to: 111 (3-3) on soft or heavy going only.

PARSONS LEGACY (IRE)
11yo b g (P J Hobbs)

Race type	NHF: 048 (0-3)
	Hdl: 3221P104P2 (2-10)
	Chs: 13216357P29215423541PF (4-22)
Conclusion:	he's effective over hurdles and fences.
Distance	2m-2m2f110y: 04833 (0-5)
	2m3f-2m5f110y: 21P1013 (3-7)
	2m6f-2m7f110y: 4217 (1-4)
	3m+: P2635P29215423541PF (2-19)
Conclusion:	he's suited by 3m or further these days.
Going	Good to firm or faster: 1223 (1-4)
	Good: 43135792151 (3-11)
	Good to soft: 31P126P24F (2-10)
	Soft/heavy: 04832P054P (0-10)
Conclusion:	he is effective when there's a little cut in the ground but seems best on good or faster going.
Fresh (absence	35 days or longer: 010167P22142351PF (4-17)
since last race)	34 days or less: 48332P14P232135954 (2-18)
Conclusion:	he seems best when fresh.

Summary of ideal conditions When running fresh (after a break of five weeks or longer) his record over hurdles or fences on good or faster going becomes: 17221351 (3-8).

PASCO (SWI)
6yo ro g (P F Nicholls)

Race type	Hdl: 211P (2-4)
	Chs: 31198 (2-5)
Conclusion:	he's effective over hurdles and fences.
Distance	2m-2m2f: 211P31198 (4-9)
	2m3f+: no runs
Conclusion:	all his runs have taken place at about 2m.
Going	Good or faster: 8 (0-1)
	Good to soft: 11P3119 (4-7)
	Soft: 2 (0-1)
	Heavy: no runs
Conclusion:	his best efforts have come on good to soft or softer going.

Course	Aintree: 8 (0-1)
	Cheltenham: P9 (0-2)
	Exeter: 3 (0-1)
	Huntingdon: 1 (1-1)
	Newbury: 2111 (3-4)

Conclusion: his four wins came on flat tracks.

Summary of ideal conditions Combine hurdle or chase starts with running on flat tracks and his record becomes: 211118 (4-6), improving to: 21111 (4-5) on good to soft or softer going, with the sole defeat coming on his hurdling debut.

PEPSYROCK (FR)

6yo b g (N J Henderson)

Race type	Chs: 6721121 (3-7)

Conclusion: he won over hurdles in France but all his runs for current trainer Nicky Henderson have taken place over fences.

Distance	2m-2m2f: 72111 (3-5)
	2m3f-2m5f: 2 (0-1)
	2m6f+: 6 (0-1)

Conclusion: he's best at about 2m.

Going	Good to firm or faster: no runs
	Good: 121 (2-3)
	Good to soft: 671 (1-3)
	Soft: 2 (0-1)
	Heavy: no runs

Conclusion: his best efforts have come on good or good to soft going.

Summary of ideal conditions Combine a distance of 2m-2m2f with running on good to soft or faster going and his record becomes: 111 (3-3)

PERCE ROCK

7yo b g (T Stack)

Race type	NHF: 14 (1-2)
	Hdl: 128911 (3-6)
	Chs: 1FF115U1 (4-8)

Conclusion: he has a 50% strike-rate over hurdles and fences.

Distance	2m-2m2f: 141281F11591 (6-12)
	2m3f-2m5f: F11U (2-4)

Conclusion: his two wins at about 2m4f came in weak races and he might prove best at 2m.

Going	Good to yielding or faster: 4F151 (2-5)
	Yielding (or good to soft): U (0-1)
	Yielding to soft: 1 (1-1)
	Soft: 891 (1-3)
	Soft to heavy: 1 (1-1)
	Heavy: 1121F (3-5)
Conclusion:	he's effective on a variety of going.
Class	Grade 1: 42F5 (0-4)
	Grade 2: 8F (0-2)
	Grade 3: 1U (1-2)
	Others: 11119111 (7-8)
Conclusion:	he has yet to score above Grade 3 level.

Summary of ideal conditions When racing in Grade 3 or lower company his record reads: 11111911U (7-9), with the first defeat coming on his 2008/2009 seasonal debut and the other when badly hampered/unseating in a 23-runner handicap chase at the Cheltenham Festival (he was going well at the time).

PLANET OF SOUND

7yo b g (P J Hobbs)

Race type	NHF: 4 (0-1)
	Hdl: 124221 (2-6)
	Chs: 41133 (2-5)
Conclusion:	he's effective over hurdles and fences.
Going	Good or faster: 313 (1-3)
	Good to soft: 221413 (2-6)
	Soft/heavy: 241 (1-3)
Conclusion:	his fast-ground win came in a maiden hurdle and he seems happiest with plenty of cut.
Track	Left-handed: 312211133 (4-9)
	Right-handed: 244 (0-3)
Conclusion:	he has yet to win on a right-handed track.
Class	1: 33 (0-2)
	2: no runs
	3: 221411 (3-6)
	4 or lower: 3124 (1-4)
Conclusion:	he has yet to win above Class 3 level but did finish third in the Arkle (a Grade 1 event) at the 2009 Cheltenham Festival.

Summary of ideal conditions Combine hurdle or chase starts with racing on a left-handed track and his record becomes: 12211133 (4-8), improving to: 122111 (4-6) if we knock out his runs in Class 1 contests.

POLITICAL PADDY
7yo b g (R Nixon)

Race type	NHF: 86 (0-2)
	Hdl: 763U24643108151 (3-15)
Conclusion:	he has yet to win over hurdles but has shown promise on several occasions.
Distance	2m-2m2f: 86 (0-2)
	2m3f-2m5f: 3405 (0-4)
	2m6f-2m7f: U264111 (3-7)
	3m+: 7638 (0-4)
Conclusion:	he seems best at about 2m6f.
Going	Good to firm: 35 (0-2)
	Good: 86461 (1-5)
	Good to soft: no runs
	Soft: 7U4108 (1-6)
	Heavy: 6231 (1-4)
Conclusion:	he runs especially well on soft/heavy going but does handle faster ground.
Headgear	Cheekpieces: 324643108151 (3-12)
	Without headgear: 8676U (0-5)
Conclusion:	his best efforts have come when wearing cheekpieces.

Summary of ideal conditions When racing over hurdles in cheekpieces his record is: 32464108151 (3-11), improving to: U264111 (3-7) at 2m6f-2m7f only.

POP (FR)
6yo b g (H D Daly)

Race type	NHF: 43 (0-2)
	Hdl: 3209311 (2-7)
	Chs: F1231FP (2-7)
Conclusion:	he's effective over hurdles and fences.
Distance	1m5f-2m4.5f: 433209311F121F (4-14)
	2m5f-2m7.5f: 3 (0-1)
	3m+ P (0-1)
Conclusion:	he struggles to stay beyond 2m4f.
Going	Good to firm or faster: no runs
	Good: 311FP (2-5)
	Good to soft: 3331F (1-5)
	Soft/heavy: 420912 (1-6)
Conclusion:	he seems effective under most conditions.

Summary of ideal conditions When racing over hurdles or fences from 2m-2m4.5f his record reads: 3209311F121F (4-12), improving to: F121F (2-5) over fences. His jumping still gives cause for concern and he is likely to prove best in small fields.

POSSOL (FR)
6yo b g (H D Daly)
Race type   Hdl: 8 (0-1)
                 Chs: 32232113201 (3-11)
Conclusion: he's best over fences.
Going   Good or faster: 321821 (2-6)
                 Good to soft: 23130 (1-5)
                 Soft/heavy: 2 (0-1)
Conclusion: he seems happiest on good to soft or faster going.
Fresh   Seasonal debuts: 38 (0-2)
Conclusion: he has yet to score at the first time of asking.
Headgear   Cheekpieces: 0 (0-1)
Conclusion: he ran poorly when tried in cheekpieces – finishing 16th of 21 at the 2009 Cheltenham Festival despite going off as a well-backed 7-1 shot.

Summary of ideal conditions When racing over fences without headgear his record reads: 3223211321 (3-10). His two most recent wins came over 3m on flat tracks.

PREISTS LEAP (IRE)
9yo b g (Thomas Gerard O'Leary)
Course   Gowran Park: 2211 (2-4)
                 Others: 04462319645F341265572477F90 (2-27)
Conclusion: he runs especially well at Gowran Park – a stiff right-handed track. His other wins came in a maiden hurdle at Thurles back in February 2005 and in a beginners chase at Limerick (March 2007) when 11-10 favourite).

Summary of ideal conditions Quite simply, he's a Gowran Park course expert, his record there being: 2211 (2-4). The latest win came when 20-1 for a valuable 3m handicap chase on heavy going.

PUNJABI
6yo b g (N J Henderson)

Race type	Hdl: 1142142311F312 (6-14)
Conclusion:	he has yet to finish out of the frame when completing the course over hurdles.
Distance	2m-2m1f: 1142142311F312 (6-14)
Conclusion:	all his hurdles runs have taken place at about 2m.
Going	Good or faster: 1211F (3-5)
	Good to soft: 44231 (1-5)
	Soft/heavy: 1132 (2-4)
Conclusion:	he handles slow going but seems best on good or faster ground.
Fresh	Seasonal debuts: 141 (2-3)
Conclusion:	he ran as though needing his reappearance run during the 2007/2008 season but scored on his other two seasonal debuts.

Summary of ideal conditions When racing over hurdles his record is: 1142142311F312 (6-14), improving to: 1211 (3-4) on good or faster going, with the sole defeat by subsequent Champion Hurdle winner Katchit.

QUASAR D'OUDAIRIES (FR)
5yo b g (Nick Williams)

Race type	Hdl: 712405641 (2-9)
Conclusion:	all his runs have taken place over hurdles but he is likely to switch to fences this season or next.
Distance	1m5f: 7 (0-1)
	2m-2m1f: 1240641 (2-7)
	2m3f+: 5 (0-1)
Conclusion:	his wins came at about 2m but his trainer expects him to stay further.
Going	Good to firm or faster: 4 (0-1)
	Good: 10 (1-2)
	Good to soft: 41 (1-2)
	Soft: 7256 (0-4)
	Heavy: no runs
Conclusion:	his best efforts have come on good or good to soft going.
Course	Chepstow: 0 (0-1)
	Exeter: 75 (0-2)
	Hereford: 1 (1-1)
	Ludlow: 4 (0-1)
	Taunton: 41 (1-2)
	Wincanton: 26 (0-2)
Conclusion:	both his wins came on easy right-handed tracks.

Fresh   Seasonal debuts: 70 (0-2)
Conclusion: he might need his first run of the season.
Summary of ideal conditions Aside from seasonal debuts, his record on good to soft or faster going reads: 1441 (2-4).

RASLAN
6yo b g (D E Pipe)
Race type   Hdl: 21120218301P0P02F72971 (5-22)
                    Chs: 4 (0-1)
Conclusion: he has a good strike-rate over hurdles and ran with credit on his chase debut at Worcester in May 2009 where he was beaten by just over three lengths into fourth place.
Distance   2m-2m1f: 212 (1-3)
                    2m2f-2m5.5f: 109 (1-3)
                    2m6f-2m7.5f: 2F41 (1-4)
                    3m+: 218301P0P0727 (2-13)
Conclusion: his recent wins have come at 2m6f or further.
Going   Good to firm or faster: 1F421 (2-5)
                    Good: 2831279 (1-7)
                    Good to soft: 100P0P07 (1-8)
                    Soft/heavy: 212 (1-3)
Conclusion: he needs fast ground. His two wins on good to soft or softer going came in weak races early in his career and even his victory on officially 'good' going (at Bangor in December 2007) came on a surface rated as 'good to firm' by Raceform.
Summary of ideal conditions When racing on good to firm or faster going (including that Bangor run) his record reads: 11F421 (3-6), improving to: 11F21 (3-5) over hurdles only, with the runner-up effort by a neck.

RIMSKY (IRE)
8yo gr g (N A Twiston-Davies)
Race type   NHF: 218 (1-3)
                    Hdl: 11064266257 (2-11)
                    Chs: 251630482383456 (1-15)
Conclusion: he's effective over hurdles and fences.
Distance   2m-2m2f: 21810 (2-5)
                    2m3f-2m5f: 16236 (1-5)
                    2m6f-3m2.5f: 642625251647885 (1-15)
                    3m4f+: 3034 (0-4)
Conclusion: his latest win came at 2m6f but he has placed in the last two runnings of the 4m Totesport Eider.

Course	Aintree: 86 (0-2)
	Bangor: 18 (1-2)
	Carlisle: 235 (0-3)
	Cheltenham: 0662078 (0-7)
	Chepstow: 112 (2-3)
	Exeter: 5 (0-1)
	Huntingdon: 4 (0-1)
	Kelso: 4 (0-1)
	Leicester: 6 (0-1)
	Newbury: 24 (0-2)
	Newcastle: 33 (0-2)
	Perth: 56 (0-2)
	Towcester: 1 (1-1)
	Wetherby: 2 (0-1)

Conclusion: he seems best on undulating tracks, his wins over obstacles having come at Chepstow (2) and Towcester.

Headgear Blinkers: 64266255756 (0-11)
Without headgear: 218110216304823834 (4-18)

Conclusion: he has yet to win when wearing headgear.

Fresh First two runs or after a break of approx 5 weeks:
21112625138283 (4-14)
Other runs: 806462560473456 (0-15)

Conclusion: he runs well when fresh.

Summary of ideal conditions When running fresh (first two runs each season or after a break of about five weeks or more) his record reads: 21112625138283 (4-14), improving to: 21112138283 (4-11) when not wearing blinkers. Given his good record at Chepstow the Welsh National would make an ideal early-season target.

RING BO REE (IRE)
6yo b g (T R George)

Race	Non-handicap hurdles: 890 (0-3)
conditions	Handicap hurdles: F124 (1-4)

Conclusion: he improved for the switch to handicap company.

Distance 2m-2m2f: 8902 (0-4)
2m3f-2m5f: F14 (1-3)

Conclusion: he's effective at 2m but seems best over further.

Going	Good to firm or faster: no runs
	Good: 1 (1-1)
	Good to soft: 82 (0-2)
	Soft: 90F4 (0-4)
	Heavy: no runs
Conclusion:	his good-ground win came when odds-on and he might prove best on slower going.

Summary of ideal conditions When racing in handicap company his record reads: F124 (1-4). From left to right: F – looked the likely winner prior to stumbling and falling on the run-in at Ludlow, 1st – won at Hereford (2m4f), 2nd – found the drop back to 2m against him when second of 16 at Cheltenham, and 4th – only beaten by around two lengths after fluffing the last at Kempton.

RING THE BOSS (IRE)
8yo b g (P J Hobbs)

Race type	NHF: 6R0 (0-3)
	Hdl: 4544811111632 (5-13)
	Chs: 2812410 (2-7)
Conclusion:	he is effective over hurdles and fences.
Distance	2m-2m2f: 6R04111628 (3-10)
	2m3f-2m5f: 458113212410 (4-12)
	2m6f+: 4 (0-1)
Conclusion:	he is effective at 2m when ground conditions are testing but is likely to prove best over longer trips.
Going	Good to firm or faster: no runs
	Good: 6451631 (2-7)
	Good to yielding: 2 (0-1)
	Good to soft: R0482840 (0-8)
	Soft: 4112 (2-4)
	Heavy: 111 (3-3)
Conclusion:	he runs especially well on soft or heavy going.
Trainer	K G Reveley: 6R045448 (0-8)
	G A Swinbank: 111 (3-3)
	P J Hobbs: 116283212410 (4-12)
Conclusion:	he was unbeaten in three outings for Alan Swinbank and has done well for Philip Hobbs.

Summary of ideal conditions Since leaving the Keith Reveley yard his record is: 111116283212410 (7-15), improving to: 111113212410 (7-12) at 2m3f or further (or at shorter trips on soft/heavy going).

ROBY DE CIMBRE (FR)
6yo gr g (P F Nicholls)

Race type	Hdl: 4449423 (0-7)
	Chs: F12112010P (4-10)
Conclusion:	he's best over fences.
Distance	2m-2m2.5f: 1211 (3-4)
(chase runs	2m3f-2m5.5f: F210P (1-5)
only)	2m6f+: 0 (0-1)
Conclusion:	most of his wins have come at about 2m but he does stay further.
Going (chase	Good to firm or faster: 121P (2-4)
runs only)	Good: 120 (1-3)
	Good to soft: no runs
	Soft/heavy: F10 (1-3)
Conclusion:	he's suited by fast ground.
Field size	16 or more runners: 0 (0-1)
(chase runs	12-15 runners: 20P (0-3)
only)	8-11 runners: 2 (0-1)
	7 or fewer runners: F1111 (4-5)
Conclusion:	all his wins have come in small fields (5, 5, 4 and 5 ran).

Summary of ideal conditions When racing over fences in fields of 11 or fewer runners his record reads: F12111 (4-6).

ROLL ALONG (IRE)
9yo b g (Carl Llewellyn)

Race type	NHF: 111 (3-3)
	Hdl: 1130 (2-4)
	Chs: 122513P64 (2-9)
Conclusion:	he's effective over hurdles and fences.
Fresh	First run of the season: 11111 (5-5)
	Second run of the season: 1123 (2-4)
	Other runs: 3025P64 (0-7)
Conclusion:	he runs especially well when fresh.

Summary of ideal conditions Best fresh, his record first time out reads: 11111 (5-5), with the wins coming at odds of: 4-1, 2-1, 13-8, 5-4 and 5-1.

RORY BOY (USA)

4yo b g (N A Twiston-Davies)

Race type	Hdl: 21227934225 (1-11)
Conclusion:	all his jumps outings have taken place over hurdles.
Distance	2m-2m2f: 2122793425 (1-10)
	2m3f-2m5f: 2 (0-1)
Conclusion:	his stamina seemed to give out when runner-up over 2m3f at Newbury last term.
Going	Good to firm or faster: 1 (1-1)
	Good: 27225 (0-5)
	Good to soft: 24 (0-2)
	Soft/heavy: 293 (0-3)
Conclusion:	he's suited by fast going.
Course	Ascot: 2 (0-1)
	Bangor: 4 (0-1)
	Cheltenham: 795 (0-3)
	Ludlow: 3 (0-1)
	Newbury: 2 (0-1)
	Perth: 12 (1-2)
	Stratford: 22 (0-2)
Conclusion:	he has a poor record at Cheltenham.

Summary of ideal conditions If we discard his runs at Cheltenham, where he simply fails to cope with the stiff/undulating track, his record reads: 21223422 (1-8), improving to: 2122 (1-4) on good or faster going, with the latest defeat by a neck.

RUBY CROWN

7yo b m (K C Bailey)

Race type	NHF: 85 (0-2)
	Hdl: 8F012153P1 (3-10)
Conclusion:	she has a 30% strike-rate over hurdles.
Distance	2m-2m2.5f: 858121531 (3-9)
	2m3f-2m5.5f: 0 (0-1)
	2m6f+: FP (0-2)
Conclusion:	all her wins have come at about 2m.
Track	Left-handed: 8F25 (0-4)
	Right-handed: 850113P1 (3-8)
Conclusion:	all her wins have come on right-handed tracks (Folkestone, Leicester and Towcester).

Summary of ideal conditions Combine right-handed hurdle starts with racing from 2m-2m2.5f and her record becomes: 1131 (3-4). She has winning form on ground ranging from good through to heavy and seems happiest on undulating tracks.

RUSSIAN TRIGGER

7yo b g (V R A Dartnall)

Race type	Hdl: 511107 (3-6)
	Chs: 3311 (2-4)
Conclusion:	he's effective over hurdles and fences.
Distance	2m-2m2f: 5 (0-1)
	2m3f-2m7.5f: 1113 (3-4)
	3m-3m1f: 073 (0-3)
	3m2f+: 11 (2-2)
Conclusion:	he appreciates a stiff test of stamina.
Going	Good or faster: no runs
	Good to soft: 1071 (2-4)
	Soft: 51131 (3-5)
	Heavy: 3 (0-1)
Conclusion:	he has avoided fast ground throughout his career.
Headgear	Cheekpieces: 73 (0-2)
Conclusion:	he ran poorly when tried in headgear – finishing seventh of 15 in a handicap hurdle at Haydock before his 23-length third on his chase debut at Exeter.

Summary of ideal conditions Combine hurdle or chase starts with racing over and his record becomes: 1110311 (5-7), with the 'duck egg' coming at the Cheltenham Festival.

SANGFROID

5yo gr g (Nick Williams)

Race type	Hdl: 23204722F1 (1-10)
Conclusion:	all his jumps runs have taken place over hurdles but novice chasing is a "possibility" according to his trainer.
Distance	2m-2m2f: 232042 (0-6)
	2m3f-2m7f: 72F1 (1-4)
Conclusion:	he improved for the step up beyond 2m.
Going	Good to firm or faster: 1 (1-1)
	Good: 30 (0-2)
	Good to soft: 247F (0-4)
	Soft/heavy: 222 (0-3)
Conclusion:	his sole win came on good to firm going but he is effective on slow ground.

Headgear   Visor: 7 (0-1)
Conclusion: he ran poorly when tried in a visor, finishing a 15-length seventh
                  of 14 at Taunton.

Summary of ideal conditions When racing over a distance of 2m3f or further,
without headgear, his record reads: 22F1 (1-4).

SEA WALL

7yo b g (Jonjo O'Neill)
Race type   Hdl: 5031718 (2-7)
                  Chs: P3150P221P (2-10)
Conclusion: he's effective over hurdles and fences.
Going   Good to firm or faster: 3P113122 (3-8)
                  Good: 507850P1P (1-9)
                  Good to soft or softer: no runs
Conclusion: he has avoided slow ground throughout his career.
Jockey   A P McCoy: 5118150221P (4-11)
                  Others: 03P73P (0-6)
Conclusion: all his wins came when ridden by Tony McCoy.
Headgear   Cheekpieces: P (0-1)
Conclusion: he ran poorly when tried in cheekpieces, pulling up in a 3m
                  handicap chase at Doncaster in December 2008.

Summary of ideal conditions When racing on good to firm or faster going his
record reads: 3P113122 (3-8), improving to: 11122 (3-5) when ridden by A P
McCoy. Both defeats came on tracks with stiff/uphill finishes – Exeter and Towcester
– and he is likely to prove best on flat/easy courses.

SEYMOUR WELD
9yo ch g (C T Pogson)

Race type	NHF: 4766 (0-4)
	Hdl: 31160321886278 (3-14)
	Chs: 242110111PF (5-11)
Conclusion:	he's a three-time winner over hurdles but has a superior strike-rate over fences.
Course	Cheltenham: 1 (1-1)
	Huntingdon: 68 (0-2)
	Market Rasen: 7611011 (4-7)
	Sedgefield: 672 (0-3)
	Southwell: 3 (0-1)
	Stratford: 3 (0-1)
	Uttoxeter: 12188242P (2-9)
	Worcester: 4160F (1-5)
Conclusion:	he has a good record at Market Rasen. His Cheltenham win was a fortunate one, as his two main market rivals – Lodge Lane and Buck The Legend – both fell.
Class	1: 0P (0-2)
	2: 1 (1-1)
	3: 1F (1-2)
	4: 603886278242111 (3-15)
	5: 31121 (3-5)
	6: 4766 (0-4)
Conclusion:	all bar one of his wins (that fortunate Cheltenham one) have come in Class 3 or lower company.
Field size (hurdle runs only)	12 or more runners: 6032886278 (0-10)
	11 or fewer runners: 3111 (3-4)
Field size (chase runs only)	12 or more runners: 0P (0-2)
	8-11 runners: 42F (0-3)
	7 or fewer runners: 211111 (5-6)
Conclusion:	he's a front-runner and is best able to dominate when racing in small fields. His cut-off point would seem to be 11 runners if racing over hurdles and seven runners in chases.

Summary of ideal conditions If we ignore his hurdle and chase debuts, when clearly in need of the experience, his record in small fields (11 or less over hurdles, seven or less over fences) becomes: 1111111 (7-7). He is likely to prove best on easy tracks such as Market Rasen and all eight of his wins came on officially good going, the latest over 3m1.5f.

SHERIFF HUTTON (IRE)
6yo b g (T D Walford)

Race type	NHF: 86 (0-2)
	Hdl: 6897113145282 (3-13)
	Chs: 1 (1-1)
Conclusion:	he was profitable to follow over hurdles (wins at 8-1, 5-1 and 9-2 from 13 starts) and made a successful chase debut at Sedgefield in May 2009.
Distance	2m-2m2.5f: 86687 (0-5)
	2m3f-2m5.5f: 911321 (3-6)
	2m6f-2m7.5f: 4 (0-1)
	3m+: 1528 (1-4)
Conclusion:	he stays an easy 3m but might prove best at 2m4f-2m6f.
Going	Good to firm or faster: 7112 (2-4)
	Good: 9182 (1-4)
	Good to soft (good in places): 1 (1-1)
	Good to soft: 683 (0-3)
	Soft/heavy: 8645 (0-4)
Conclusion:	he prefers fast ground.

Summary of ideal conditions Combine a distance of 2m3f or further with racing on ground faster than good to soft and his record becomes: 91112821 (4-8). The ninth place came on his hurdles debut when no doubt in need of the experience and the other unplaced effort came over a stiff 3m at Newcastle.

SILVERBURN (IRE)
8yo b g (P F Nicholls)

Race type	NHF: 21 (1-2)
	Hdl: 21146 (2-5)
	Chs: 231464PP (1-8)
Conclusion:	he's effective over hurdles and fences.
Distance	2m-2m2f: 21114 (3-5)
	2m3f-2m5f: 24216P (1-6)
	3m+: 634P (0-4)
Conclusion:	all his wins have come over trips short of 3m.
Going	Good or faster: 26P (0-3)
	Good to soft: 4234P (0-5)
	Soft/heavy: 2111164 (4-7)
Conclusion:	he seems best on soft or heavy going.
Fresh	Seasonal debuts: 2226 (0-4)
Conclusion:	he might need his first run of the season.

Course	Cheltenham: 446P (0-4)
Conclusion:	he has yet to reach the first three at Cheltenham.

Summary of ideal conditions If we ignore his seasonal debuts and runs at Cheltenham his record at 2m-2m5f becomes: 11114 (4-5).

SIMON

10yo b g (J L Spearing)

Race type	Hdl: 1224273 (1-7)
	Ch: 434121152611F52U4U47P (5-21)
Conclusion:	he's best over fences.
Distance	2m-2m2f110y: 142 (1-3)
	2m3f-2m6f110y: 27343412 (1-8)
	3m+: 21152611F52U4U47P (4-11)
Conclusion:	he's best over 3m or further. His 2m5f Wincanton win (21 January 2006) was a most fortunate one as he was held in third place when left clear by two fallers.
Going	Good or faster: 4F524U (0-6)
	Good to soft: 715U7P (1-6)
	Soft: 1222343126114 (4-13)
	Heavy: 421 (1-3)
Conclusion:	he's best on good to soft or softer going.
Fresh	Seasonal debuts: 14554 (1-5)
Conclusion:	he won on his racecourse debut in Ireland when trained by Philip Fenton but has finished well beaten in all his reappearance efforts for current trainer John Spearing.
Track (chase starts only)	Flat: 4341211511F4U (5-13)
	Significant undulations: 2652U47P (0-8)
Conclusion:	he seems best on flat tracks.

Summary of ideal conditions Combine chase starts with racing at 3m or further, outside of his seasonal debuts, and his record becomes: 112611F2U4U7P (4-13), improving to: 1111 (4-4) on flat tracks and on good to soft or softer going.

SIR HARRY ORMESHER
6yo b g (A King)

Race type	NHF: 610 (1-3)
	Hdl: 1412 (2-4)
	Chs: 14 (1-2)
Conclusion:	he has winning form over hurdles and fences.
Distance	1m4.5f: 6 (0-1)
	2m-2m3f: 101411 (4-6)
	2m4f-2m6f: 24 (0-2)
Conclusion:	he has yet to win beyond 2m3f.
Going	Good to firm or faster: 4 (0-1)
	Good: 11 (2-2)
	Good to soft: 101 (2-3)
	Soft: 4 (0-1)
	Heavy: 26 (0-2)
Conclusion:	he has yet to impress when racing on extremes of going.
Class	1: 044 (0-3)
	2 or lower: 611121 (4-6)
Conclusion:	he struggled when tried in Class 1 company.

Summary of ideal conditions Since finishing an outpaced sixth of 17 when 50-1 for a junior bumper at Newbury on his debut, his record reads: 10141214 (4-8), improving to: 1111 (4-4) if we knock out his runs in Class 1 company and those on heavy going.

SNAP TIE (IRE)
7yo b g (P J Hobbs)

Race type	NHF: 1262 (1-4)
	Hdl: 122312376 (2-9)
Conclusion:	he has reached the first three places in ten of his 13 career outings.
Going	Good or faster: 11221236 (3-8)
	Good to soft: 26237 (0-5)
	Soft/heavy: no runs
Conclusion:	he needs fast ground.
Course	Ayr: 6 (0-1)
	Cheltenham: 2612227 (1-7)
	Haydock: 3 (0-1)
	Kempton: 12 (1-2)
	Limerick: 1 (1-1)
	Newbury: 2 (0-1)
Conclusion:	he seems best on flat tracks. He won a maiden hurdle at Cheltenham when 6-4 favourite but his other six runs there have resulted in defeat.

Fresh (absence   42 days or longer: 12213127 (3-8)
since last race)   28-41 days: 226 (0-3)
                    27 days or less: 63 (0-2)
Conclusion: he runs best when fresh.
Summary of ideal conditions When running fresh (after a break of six weeks or longer) his record reads: 12213127 (3-8), improving to: 1212 (2-4) away from Cheltenham, with the first defeat coming in a 22-runner bumper and the other by three-quarters of a length in the Grade 1 Christmas Hurdle at Kempton.

SOMETHING WELLS (FR)
8yo b g (Miss Venetia Williams)
Race type   Hdl: 34 (0-2)
                    Chs: 112F2202721 (3-11)
Conclusion: he's best over fences.
Distance   2m-2m2.5f: 1220 (1-4)
                    2m3f-2m4.5f: 1F21 (2-4)
                    2m5f-2m7.5f: 3422 (0-4)
                    3m+: 7 (0-1)
Conclusion: he's best at about 2m4f.
Going   Good to firm or faster: no runs
                    Good: 4 (0-1)
                    Good (good to soft in places): 12 (1-2)
                    Good to soft: 2F20271 (1-7)
                    Soft: 31 (1-2)
                    Heavy: 2 (0-1)
Conclusion: he seems most effective when there's cut in the ground.
Track   Left-handed: 312F2221 (2-8)
                    Right-handed: 41027 (1-5)
Conclusion: he earned the comment 'jumped left throughout' when successful at right-handed Taunton in January 2008 and repeated that trait when beaten three times on right-handed tracks last winter.
Summary of ideal conditions When racing on ground slower than good his record over trips short of 3m reads: 3112F220221 (3-11). On left-handed tracks only, his slow-ground form below 3m becomes: 12F2221 (2-7). From left-to-right: 1st – made a winning chase debut in handicap company at Uttoxeter (2m), 2nd – beaten by six lengths at Cheltenham (2m5f), F – fell in the 2008 running of the Jewson Novices' Handicap Chase at the Cheltenham Festival (2m4.5f), 2nd – beaten by a shorthead at Chepstow (2m), 2nd of 14 – beaten by just over three lengths at Haydock, 2nd – beaten by six lengths at Chepstow (2m3.5f), and 1st – beat 22 others in the 2009 Jewson despite starting at odds of 33-1 (2m4.5f).

SOUTH O'THE BORDER

7yo b g (Miss Venetia Williams)

Race type	Hdl: 1341623521 (3-10)
	Chs: 4 (0-1)
Conclusion:	he's best over hurdles.
Distance	2m-2m2.5f: 134142 (2-6)
	2m3f-2m5.5f: 6321 (1-4)
	2m6f+: 5 (0-1)
Conclusion:	he didn't seem to stay the trip when fifth over 2m6.5f at Uttoxeter last term.
Going	Good to firm or faster: no runs
	Good: 421 (1-3)
	Good to soft: 1635 (1-4)
	Soft/heavy: 3412 (1-4)
Conclusion:	his soft-ground win came in a weak affair and he's likely to prove best on good to soft or faster going.
Track	Left-handed: 4652 (0-4)
	Right-handed: 131231 (3-6)
	Figure-of-eight: 4 (0-1)
Conclusion:	three of his four Flat wins came on right-handed tracks and his jumps form is following a similar pattern.

Summary of ideal conditions When racing right-handed his record reads: 131231 (3-6), improving to: 131 (2-3) on good to soft or faster going only.

SPANISH CRUISE (IRE)

5yo gr g (Andrew Turnell)

Race type	NHF: 166 (1-3)
	Hdl: 48F05514 (1-8)
Conclusion:	he won a bumper on his debut and was ending a losing run by scoring over hurdles at Wincanton in March 2009.
Going	Good to firm or faster: 14 (1-2)
	Good: no runs
	Good to soft: 485 (0-3)
	Soft/heavy: 6F05 (0-4)
	Polytrack: 16 (1-2)
Conclusion:	his best efforts have come on fast surfaces.

Summary of ideal conditions When racing on good/faster turf or Polytrack his record reads: 1614 (2-4). His latest win came at right-handed Wincanton (2m4f) but he jumped out to his left when a beaten favourite at Huntingdon next time out and there might be further improvement to come when he encounters the combination of a left-handed track and fast going.

STAN (NZ)
10yo b g (Tim Vaughan)

Race type	Hdl: 3241201640 (2-10)
	Chs: 133P32U6F37251142P51P04PF (4-25)
Conclusion:	he's effective over hurdles and fences.
Distance	2m-2m2.5f: 24202U60F31425 (1-14)
	2m3f-2m5.5f: 3116143P371P1P4P (5-16)
	2m6f+: 3250F (0-5)
Conclusion:	he's effective at 2m but best at about 2m4f.
Going	Good to firm or faster: 11 (2-2)
	Good: 2014U60F214204 (2-14)
	Good to soft: 23511PF (2-7)
	Soft: 363P3237P5 (0-10)
	Heavy: 4P (0-2)
Conclusion:	he needs good to soft or faster going.
Field size	14 or more runners: 3210660F11P104PF (4-16)
	12-13 runners: 432P (0-4)
	11 or fewer runners: 211433P32U72545 (2-15)
Conclusion:	he sometimes pulls too hard and seems best suited to racing in large fields.
Time of year	Jan: 2321P (1-5)
	Feb: 504 (0-3)
	Mar: 02UP (0-4)
	Apr: 166114F (3-7)
	May: 10 (1-2)
	Jun-Sep: no runs
	Oct: 3243F2 (0-6)
	Nov: 433P (0-4)
	Dec: 1P75 (1-4)
Conclusion:	he tends to peak in the spring.
Headgear	Blinkers: 32U60F37 (0-8)
	Without headgear: 324120161433P251142P51P04PF (6-27)
Conclusion:	he has yet to win when wearing headgear.

Summary of ideal conditions Combine chases of 2m-2m5.5f with racing on good to soft or faster going, in fields of 12 or more runners, without headgear, and his record becomes: 11214P (3-6).

STRAWBERRY (IRE)
8yo b m (J W Mullins)

Race type	NHF: 2427 (0-4)
	Hdl: 2P31018366 (2-10)
	Chs: P522215133 (2-10)
Conclusion:	she's effective over hurdles and fences.
Going	Good or faster: 4221832625633 (1-13)
	Good to soft or softer: 7P310P5211 (3-10)
	Polytrack: 2 (0-1)
Conclusion:	her fast-ground win came when 5-4 favourite and she seems most effective on good to soft or softer going.
Time of year	Jan: 6 (0-1)
	Feb: 3213 (1-4)
	Mar-Apr: 2421018213 (3-10)
	May-Oct: 5 (0-1)
	Nov-Dec: 72P3P526 (0-8)
Conclusion:	she tends to peak in the second half of the jumps season.

Summary of ideal conditions Combine hurdle or chase starts with racing on good to soft or softer going and her record becomes: P310P5211 (3-9), improving to: 310211 (3-6) when only considering her runs from 1 February until the end of the season.

SUPREME DUKE (IRE)
7yo br g (P J Hobbs)

Race type	NHF: 2 (0-1)
	Hdl: 831F9 (1-5)
	Chs: 4133 (1-4)
Conclusion:	he's effective over hurdles and fences.
Going	Good to firm or faster: no runs
	Good: 2831F4133 (2-9)
	Good to soft: 9 (0-1)
	Soft/heavy: no runs
Conclusion:	most of his runs have taken place on good going.
Track	Left-handed: 8F (0-2)
	Right-handed: 23194133 (2-8)
Conclusion:	he has yet to prove effective on a left-handed track.

Summary of ideal conditions Combine a right-handed track with racing on good or faster going and his record becomes: 2314133 (2-7). He's effective from 2m-2m4f and is likely to prove best in small fields (his wins came against just four and five rivals).

TARANIS (FR)
6yo ch g (P F Nicholls)

Race type	Hdl: 13114 (3-5)
	Chs: 1U111F3121 (6-10)
Conclusion:	he is effective over hurdles and fences.
Fresh (absence	35 days or longer: 1111111 (7-7)
since last race)	34 days or less: 3U11F324 (2-8)
Conclusion:	he runs especially well when fresh (his two non-fresh wins came when a short-priced favourite for novice events).

Summary of ideal conditions When racing over hurdles or fences his UK record is: 131U1111F311214 (9-15), improving to: 1111111 (7-7) when rested for five weeks or longer. He seems best at trips of about 2m4f.

TARTAK (FR)
6yo b g (T R George)

Race type	Chs: 11232151 (4-8)
Conclusion:	he has a 50% strike-rate over fences.
Distance	2m-2m2.5f: 5 (0-1)
	2m3f-2m5.5f: 113211 (4-6)
	3m+: 2 (0-1)
Conclusion:	he seems best at about 2m4f.
Going	Good to firm or faster: no runs
	Good: 1 (1-1)
	Good to soft: 12315 (2-5)
	Soft: 12 (1-2)
	Heavy: no runs
Conclusion:	he has yet to race on extremes of going.
Track	Flat: 112211 (4-6)
	Significant undulations: 35 (0-2)
Conclusion:	he has twice disappointed at Cheltenham, finishing a 13-length third of five in a Grade 2 novices' chase before his 10-length fifth in the Arkle.

Summary of ideal conditions When racing on flat tracks over trips short of 3m his record reads: 11211 (4-5), with the runner-up effort excusable as he raced too keenly at Haydock.

TATENEN (FR)

5yo b g (P F Nicholls)

Race type	Hdl: 1124 (2-4)
	Chs: 112F25 (2-6)
Conclusion:	he won twice over fixed brush hurdles in France then, after a couple of disappointing runs over timber for Paul Nicholls, improved for the switch to fences.
Fresh	First two runs each season or after a break of 6 weeks+:
	112411F (4-7)
	Other runs: 225 (0-3)
Conclusion:	he's best when fresh.

Summary of ideal conditions When running fresh over fixed brush hurdles or fences his record reads: 1111F (4-5). All his runs have taken place at about 2m on good to soft or softer going.

THE REAL DEAL (IRE)

8yo b g (Nick Williams)

Race type	Non-handicap hurdles: 0421 (1-4)
	Handicap hurdles: 0160 (1-4)
	Non-handicap chases: F5P4 (0-4)
	Handicap chases: P11U046 (2-7)
Conclusion:	he is effective over hurdles and fences.
Distance	2m-2m1f: 420 (0-3)
	2m2f-2m5f: 0160F1U (2-7)
	3m+: 15P4P1046 (2-9)
Conclusion:	he is effective at about 2m4f but seems best over 3m or further.
Going	Good or faster: 4F5PU04 (0-7)
	Good to soft: 020164116 (3-9)
	Soft: 1P (1-2)
	Heavy: 0 (0-1)
Conclusion:	he's best on good to soft or softer going.
Fresh (absence since last race)	42 days or longer: 0421F10 (2-7)
	35-41 days: 01 (1-2)
	28-34 days: 416 (1-3)
	27 days or less: 605PPU4 (0-7)
Conclusion:	he runs well when fresh, all his wins coming after a break of at least four weeks.

Summary of ideal conditions When running fresh (after a break of at least four weeks) his record becomes: 042011F41106 (4-12), improving to: 1116 (3-4) in handicap company and on good to soft or softer going only.

THE SAWYER (BEL)
9yo ch g (R H Buckler)

Race type	
	NHF: 123 (1-3)
	Hdl: 258442115769 (2-12)
	Chs: 5623133U5411545F26 (3-18)

Conclusion: he's effective over hurdles and fences.

Distance	
	2m-2m2.5f: 123 (1-3)
	2m3f-2m5f: 25411762312 (3-11)
	2m5.5f+: 8425956133U541545F6 (2-19)

Conclusion: though twice a winner at 3m he seems best at about 2m4f.

Going	
	Good or faster: 263F (0-4)
	Good to soft: 125449523355 (1-12)
	Soft: 382161U4126 (3-11)
	Heavy: 157154 (2-6)

Conclusion: he needs soft or heavy going – his sole win on anything faster came in a Towcester bumper back in March 2004.

Time of year	
	Jan: 811611 (4-6)
	Feb: 52354 (0-5)
	Mar: 17135 (2-5)
	Apr: 263F2 (0-5)
	May-Jun: 6 (0-1)
	Jul-Aug: no runs
	Sep-Oct: no runs
	Nov-Dec: 32544295U54 (0-11)

Conclusion: he has a good record during January.

Summary of ideal conditions When racing on soft or heavy going his record reads: 382115761U4115426 (5-17), improving to: 11712 (3-5) at 2m3f-2m5f only.

THE VERY MAN (IRE)
7yo b g (Jonjo O'Neill)

Race type	
	NHF: 1 (1-1)
	Hdl: 224216P94120 (2-12)
	Chs: PP (0-2)

Conclusion: he didn't take to fences, jumping poorly and pulling up at Newbury (November 2007) and Haydock (March 2008).

Distance	
	2m-2m2.5f: 122PP (1-5)
	2m3f-2m6f: 426 (0-3)
	2m7f+: 1P94120 (2-7)

Conclusion: he improved for the step up beyond 2m6f.

Going	Good or faster: 49 (0-2)
	Good to soft: 2PPP0 (0-5)
	Soft: 1221612 (3-7)
	Heavy: 4 (0-1)
Conclusion:	he's best in the mud.
Track	Sharp: 42112 (2-5)
	Galloping: 122P6PP940 (1-10)
Conclusion:	he has a good record on sharp tracks – his two wins over hurdles came at Lingfield and Bangor.

Summary of ideal conditions When racing on soft or heavy going his record reads: 12216412 (3-8), improving to: 1112 (3-4) if we discard his hurdle runs at trip below 2m7f and those on galloping tracks. His wins over hurdles have come in small fields (10 and 11 ran).

THEATRE DIVA (IRE)

8yo b m (Miss Venetia Williams)

Race type	NHF: 20947 (0-5)
	Hdl: 25024323764120212121163 (4-21)
	Chs: 121BU9F (2-7)
Conclusion:	she took a while to break her duck but has now won six of her last 17 starts.
Distance	2m-2m2.5f: 20947024764120121 (3-17)
	2m3f-2m5.5f: 253232121U9F13 (3-14)
	2m6f+: B6 (0-2)
Conclusion:	she looked a non-stayer when sixth of eight in a 3m hurdle at Kempton last term.
Trainer	D T Hughes (IRE): 2094725024323764 (0-16)
	H D Daly (GB): 1202121 (3-7)
	Miss Venetia Williams (GB): 121BU9F163 (3-10)
Conclusion:	she has a good record since arriving in Britain from Ireland.
Track (British runs only)	Left-handed: 20BU93 (0-6)
	ight-handed: 12121121F16 (6-11)
Conclusion:	she runs especially well on right-handed tracks.
Field size (chase runs only)	12 or more runners: BU9 (0-3)
	10-11 runners: F (0-1)
	9 or fewer runners: 121 (2-3)
Conclusion:	her chase wins came in small fields.

Summary of ideal conditions When racing right-handed in Britain her record at 2m-2m5.5f reads: 12121121F1 (6-10). Five of her six wins came on good to soft or softer going and she has scored at least once during December/January in each of the past three seasons.

THEATRICAL MOMENT (USA)
6yo b g (Jonjo O'Neill)

Race type	NHF: 1111 (4-4)
	Hdl: 224047217 (1-9)
Conclusion:	he was unbeaten in four bumpers and finally got off the mark over hurdles in March 2009. He is expected to make his debut over fences sooner rather than later.
Distance	2m-2m2.5f: 11112244 (4-8)
	2m3f-2m6.5f: 07 (0-2)
	3m+: 217 (1-3)
Conclusion:	he improved for the step up to 3m+ last season.
Going	Good or faster: 112204717 (3-9)
	Good to soft: 142 (1-3)
	Soft: 1 (1-1)
	Heavy: no runs
Conclusion:	his soft-ground win came when 4-9 favourite for a Market Rasen bumper and he needs good ground according to his trainer.
Track (hurdle runs only)	Left-handed: 2477 (0-4)
	Right-handed: 20421 (1-5)
Conclusion:	he might prove best right-handed.

Summary of ideal conditions When racing in bumpers or over trips of 3m+ his record reads: 1111217 (5-7), improving to: 1121 (3-4) on right-handed tracks, with the sole defeat by a nose.

TIME FOR RUPERT (IRE)
5yo ch g (P R Webber)

Race type	NHF: 18 (1-2)
	Hdl: 71101 (3-5)
Conclusion:	he has won 60% of his hurdle starts and is regarded as a future chaser.
Distance	2m-2m2.5f: 187 (1-3)
	2m3f-2m5.5f: 110 (2-3)
	3m+: 1 (1-1)
Conclusion:	he improved for the step up beyond 2m.
Going	Good to firm or faster: no runs
	Good: 101 (2-3)
	Good to soft: 71 (1-2)
	Soft: 81 (1-2)
	Heavy: no runs
Conclusion:	he has yet to race on extremes of going.

Course	Aintree: 1 (1-1)
	Catterick: 1 (1-1)
	Huntingdon: 1 (1-1)
	Ludlow: 1 (1-1)
	Newbury: 7 (0-1)
	Sandown: 80 (0-2)
Conclusion:	he twice disappointed at Sandown (a stiff/galloping track) and might prove best on sharp/easy courses.

Summary of ideal conditions When racing over 2m3f or further his record reads: 1101 (3-4), improving to: 111 (3-3) if we discard his runs on stiff tracks.

TOT O'WHISKEY
8yo b g (J M Jefferson)

Race type	NHF: 11100 (3-5)
	Hdl: 11257390 (2-8)
	Chs: 212330P4 (1-8)
Conclusion:	he's effective over hurdles and fences.
Distance	2m-2m2.5f: 1110012 (4-7)
	2m3f-2m5.5f: 173902234 (1-9)
	3m+: 5130P (1-5)
Conclusion:	he's effective over a variety of trips.
Course	Aintree: 9P (0-2)
	Ayr: 4 (0-1)
	Carlisle: 212 (1-3)
	Catterick: 11 (2-2)
	Cheltenham: 030 (0-3)
	Doncaster: 57 (0-2)
	Hexham: 111 (3-3)
	Punchestown: 0 (0-1)
	Sandown: 30 (0-2)
	Towcester: 2 (0-1)
	Wetherby: 3 (0-1)
Conclusion:	he runs well at Hexham and Carlisle, two of the stiffest tracks in the country.
Fresh	First run of the season: 112 (2-3)
	Second run of the season: 111 (3-3)
	Third run of the season: 122 (1-3)
	Fourth or subsequent runs: 0057390330P4 (0-12)
Conclusion:	his wins have come early in the season.

Class   1: 0053904 (0-7)
                          2: 7023P (0-5)
                          3: 213 (1-3)
                          4 or lower: 111112 (5-6)
Conclusion: he has yet to score above Class 3 level.
Summary of ideal conditions When only considering his first three starts each
season his record becomes: 111112212 (6-9), with the latest defeat by a head. He
has winning form on ground ranging from good through to heavy.

TRAMANTANO
10yo b g (N A Twiston-Davies)
Race type   Hdl: 14440521209 (2-11)
                          Chs: 1F2PP628732125434 (2-17)
Conclusion: he's a dual winner over hurdles and fences.
Distance   2m-2m2.5f: 1444051201F2PP28732125434 (4-25)
                          2m3f+: 296 (0-3)
Conclusion: he's best at about 2m.
Going   Good or faster: 44022P27323 (0-11)
                          Good to soft: 451291P6844 (2-11)
                          Soft: 1F125 (2-5)
                          Heavy: 0 (0-1)
Conclusion: he's best on good to soft or softer going.
Fresh   First run of the season: 11212 (3-5)
                          Second run of the season: 40F1 (1-4)
                          Third or subsequent runs: 4405292PP6287325434 (0-19)
Conclusion: he scored on his racecourse debut at Windsor for Henry Candy
                          (25-1) and all his jumps wins have come first or second time out.
Summary of ideal conditions When running fresh (first two runs each season) his
record reads: 141201F21 (4-9), improving to: 1121 (3-4) if we only consider his
seasonal debuts on good to soft or softer going. The runner-up effort came in a
19-runner Grade 3 handicap hurdle when a 50-1 shot on his first start for two years.

TRICKY TRICKSTER (IRE)
6yo b g (P F Nicholls)

Race type	Ptp: 1 (1-1)
	Hdl: 42 (0-2)
	Chs: 2121 (2-4)
Conclusion:	he's best over fences.
Distance	2m4f-2m7.5f: 4222 (0-4)
	3m-3m2.5f+: 11 (2-2)
	4m+: 1 (1-1)
Conclusion:	he needs at least 3m and stays marathon trips.
Going	Good or faster: no runs
	Good to yielding: 1 (1-1)
	Good to soft: 421 (1-3)
	Soft: 21 (1-2)
	Heavy: 2 (0-1)
Conclusion:	he is suited by plenty of cut in the ground.

Summary of ideal conditions Combine chase starts with racing over 3m or further and his record becomes: 111 (3-3).

TURKO (FR)
7yo gr g (P F Nicholls)

Race type	Hdl: 1221652 (2-7)
	Chs: 11217PP123F49P8P (4-16)
Conclusion:	he's effective over hurdles and fences.
Going:	Good to firm or faster: P4 (0-2)
	Good: 165211PF (3-8)
	Good to soft: 221713PP (2-8)
	Yielding to soft: 2 (0-1)
	Soft/heavy: 2198 (1-4)
Conclusion:	his three good-ground wins came when favourite for weak events and he might prove best on good to soft or softer going.

Track	Aintree (Mildmay): 51PP (1-4)
	Aintree (National): F (0-1)
	Cheltenham: 2262739P8 (0-9)
	Chepstow: 2 (0-1)
	Fontwell: 1 (1-1)
	Leopardstown: 2 (0-1)
	Newbury: 1 (1-1)
	Sandown: 1 (1-1)
	Wetherby: P4 (0-2)
	Wincanton: 11 (2-2)
Conclusion:	he has a moderate record at Cheltenham and seems happiest on flat tracks such as Newbury and Wincanton.
Class	Grade 1: 265723 (0-6)
	Grade 2: 12PP4 (1-5)
	Grade 3: F98 (0-3)
	Others: 1212111PP (5-9)
Conclusion:	he has yet to score in Grade 1 company.
Field size	12 or more runners: 7F9P8P (0-6)
(chase starts	8-11 runners: P23 (0-3)
only	7 or fewer runners: 1121P14 (4-7)
Conclusion:	he has yet to win a big-field chase.

Summary of ideal conditions His record for Paul Nicholls, below Grade 1 company, stands at: 12121121PP1F49P8P (6-17) These figures can be improved to: 111111 (6-6) if we knock out the Cheltenham runs, those on fast ground and his chase starts in fields of 12 or more runners.

VICTORY GUNNER (IRE)
11yo ch g (C Roberts)

Race type	NHF: 8520 (0-4)
	Hdl: 5P1912996316179058 (4-18)
	Chs: F3516P434PP7P41436P7611965839P1P (5-32)
Conclusion:	he's a multiple winner over hurdles and fences.
Time of year	Jan: 96P419P (1-7)
	Feb: 51794361 (2-8)
	Mar: 220436P (0-7)
	Apr: 095PP (0-5)
	May-Sep: 59 (0-2)
	Oct: 68P758 (0-6)
	Nov: P31F3P7 (1-7)
	Dec: 816151416139 (5-12)
Conclusion:	eight of his nine career wins came during the period 26 December – 19 February.

Field size	12 or more runners: FP44P7P4P96839PP (0-16)
(chase starts	11 or fewer runners: 35163P4136761151 (5-16)
only)	

Conclusion: all his chase wins have come in small fields.

Summary of ideal conditions When racing over fences in fields of 11 or fewer runners his record reads: 35163P4136761151 (5-16), improving to: 1631111 (5-7) from late December until mid-February.

WISE MEN SAY (IRE)

7yo br g (C L Tizzard)

Race type	NHF: 310 (1-3)
	Hdl: 5731517B33 (2-10)
	Chs: P4 (0-2)

Conclusion: he has yet to win a chase but wasn't disgraced when beaten by around 10 lengths into fourth at Stratford in May 2009 and might yet make the grade over fences.

Distance	2m-2m2.5f: 310711B33 (3-9)
	2m3f-2m5.5f: 5374 (0-4)
	2m6f+: P5 (0-2)

Conclusion: he's best at about 2m.

Going	Good to firm or faster: 7PB (0-3)
	Good: 3334 (0-4)
	Good to soft: 1031 (2-4)
	Soft/heavy: 5517 (1-4)

Conclusion: he's suited by good to soft or softer going.

Summary of ideal conditions Combine a distance of 2m-2m2.5f with racing on good to soft or softer going and his record becomes: 1011 (3-4).

Glossary

Form Figures

1   First
2   Second
3   Third, etc
0   tenth or worse (sometimes referred to as a 'duck egg')
U   Unseated rider
P   Pulled-up
F   Fell
S   Slipped-up
R   Refused or ran out
B   Brought Down
C   Carried Out

The figures in brackets after a string of form figures represent the total wins/runs for a particular category. For example: Good to soft: 123U1 (2-5) – the horse in question has had five runs on good to soft going recording figures of first, second, third, unseated rider and first, a total of two wins from five runs.

Race type

Ptp	Point-to-point race
NHF	National Hunt Flat race (also called bumpers) – a race for horses aged seven or under who have not run under any recognised Rules of Racing except in National Hunt Flat races in Great Britain or in Irish National Hunt Flat races
Hdl	Hurdle race
Chs	Chase (also referred to as a race 'over fences')

Distance

6f	Six furlongs (eight furlongs = one mile, 220 yards = one furlong)
2m	Two miles
2m4.5f	Two miles four-and-a-half furlongs

Track

LH	Left-handed (the horses race in an anti-clockwise direction)
RH	Right-handed (the horses race clockwise)
F8	Figure-of-eight (the horses race both left-handed and right-handed)

Class

Pattern company	The collective term for Grade 1, 2, 3 and Listed races

Index

BERMUDA POINTE (IRE)	Fresh (especially first time out), good to soft or faster going
BERNARD (GB)	2m6f+, preferably on fast ground at Exeter and in a big field
BESHABAR (IRE)	All starts
BIBLE LORD (IRE)	Chases of 11 or fewer runners, preferably on good to soft or softer at 2m4f
BIG FELLA THANKS (GB)	3m+, good to soft or softer going (preferably soft or heavy), might prove best left-handed
BIG ZEB (IRE)	2m-2m1f, preferably in a small field
BLUEBERRY BOY (IRE)	Punchestown, preferably on soft or heavy
BRIAREUS (GB)	Good to soft or faster going, preferably at 2m-2m3f and below Grade 1 level
BRIERY FOX (IRE)	Fast ground
BUCK THE LEGEND (IRE)	2m3f+ (preferably 2m3f-2m6f), small fields, ideally below Class 1 level
BUSY ISIT (GB)	Good to soft or faster going, preferably right-handed, at 2m-2m5f and when fresh
BY GEORGE (IRE)	Right-handed
CAN'T BUY TIME (IRE)	3m+ (preferably 3m-3m1f), ideally on good to soft or faster going in a small field
CAPE TRIBULATION (GB)	Ground softer than good, preferably in hock-deep mud on a flat track
CARRICKBOY (IRE)	2m-2m2f, preferably on soft or heavy going
CARRUTHERS (GB)	Consider all runs, though preferably second start onwards, 2m3f+, soft or heavy going and away from Cheltenham

CATCH ME (GER)	Yielding to soft or softer going, preferably at trips below 3m
CHARACTER BUILDING (IRE)	Good or softer going, ideally at 3m+ on a stiff track
CHARMAINE WOOD (GB)	Right-handed, preferably at 2m on good or softer going
CLOUDY LANE (GB)	2m4f+ (probably not stay 3m4f+), ideally from second start onwards and not on tight
COE (IRE)	Soft or heavy going, 2m3f+ (ideally 3m+), preferably on a left-handed track
CONSIGLIERE (FR)	Blinkers, preferably in small fields, at 2m-2m4f and on soft or heavy going
COPPER BLEU (IRE)	All starts, though preferably on soft or heavy going on a galloping track
CORNAS (NZ)	Consider all starts, though might prove best right-handed
CRESCENT ISLAND (IRE)	Fields of 12 or more runners, 2m-2m5.5f, preferably on good ground
CRUCHAIN (IRE)	Good to soft or softer going, preferably after a recent run
DARKNESS (GB)	Chase on good to soft or faster going, preferably when ridden by A P McCoy
DEEP PURPLE (GB)	Consider all starts, though likely to prove best left-handed, in small fields and on fast
DEFINITY (IRE)	All starts, though preferably over 3m+
DIZZY FUTURE (GB)	April or May, preferably over 3m+
DOM D'ORGEVAL (FR)	Handicap hurdles, preferably left-handed, at 2m4f+, without headgear and on soft/heavy going

DUC DE REGNIERE (FR)   First two runs each season

EARTH PLANET (IRE)   Big fields, preferably at about 2m4f when ridden
                              by Ruby Walsh

EL DANCER (GER)   Second start onwards, left-handed, preferably on
                              good or softer going

ELZAHANN (IRE)   Good or faster going, preferably at 3m+ in the
                              spring

ENGLISHTOWN (FR)   Handicap hurdles, left-handed, good or faster
                              going

FINGER ONTHE PULSE (IRE)   2m-2m5.5f, preferably from March to October
                              when fresh

FIRE AND RAIN (FR)   Chases, good or faster going, might prove best
                              left-handed in spring/summer

FIRST LOOK (FR)   Ayr, 2m-2m4f

FLAKE (GB)   Fields of seven or fewer runners

FORPADYDEPLASTERER (IRE)   Consider all starts, though likely to prove best in
                              big fields, especially at 2m

FORTUNATE DAVE (USA)   Cheekpieces, preferably right-handed (especially
                              Market Rasen & Huntingdon) at trips of about
                              2m6f

FRONTIER DANCER (IRE)   Trips of about 2m

FUNDAMENTALIST (IRE)   Hurdles or small-field chases, good to soft or
                              faster going

GARDE CHAMPETRE (FR)   Cross-country races, preferably when ridden by
                              Nina Carberry

GAUVAIN (GER)   Small-field chases

GREEN GAMBLE (GB)	Chases of 2m-2m1.5f, no headgear, ideally in small field and on a sharp track
GREENBRIDGE (IRE)	Good to soft or faster going, preferably in the spring and on sharp tracks
HELLO BUD (IRE)	Chases, preferably when returned to the track within four weeks of a win
HENNESSY (IRE)	Fresh
I HAVE DREAMED (IRE)	2m, fresh
IMPERIAL COMMANDER (IRE)	Chases of about 2m4f
I'MSINGINGTHEBLUES (IRE)	Fresh, 2m, preferably on fast going
JAUNTY FLIGHT (GB)	2m3f+, soft or heavy going
JOE LIVELY (IRE)	Small fields, preferably on soft or heavy going
KALAHARI KING (FR)	Good to soft or faster going, preferably left-handed
KATIES TUITOR (GB)	Big fields (12+), preferably right-handed
KEENAN'S FUTURE (IRE)	Left-handed chases, preferably in small fields on good to soft or softer going
KEEPITSECRET (IRE)	Spring/summer, good or faster going (preferably good to firm or faster), 2m3f+ (ideally 3m+)
KEMPSKI (GB)	Ayr hurdles, preferably at 2m4f on heavy going, in small fields and after a recent run
KEW JUMPER (IRE)	Chases, March-April, ideally on good or faster going
KNOWHERE (IRE)	Fresh, preferably in small fields, below Grade 1 level and at trips below 3m2f

KORNATI KID (GB)	Right-handed, preferably on slow going
LASKARI (FR)	Chases of about 2m4f, preferably when fresh (might also prove best right-handed on decent going)
L'AVENTURE (FR)	Good to soft or softer going (ideally soft or heavy), small fields
LE BURF (FR)	Right-handed, ideally at 2m3f+ unless racing on soft/heavy going
LIGHTNING STRIKE (GER)	Small fields
LODGE LANE (IRE)	Tracks other than Cheltenham, preferably when not wearing headgear
MADISON DU BERLAIS (FR)	Flat tracks, preferably when wearing cheekpieces, in a small field & after a recent run
MALJIMAR (IRE)	Fresh
MON MOME (FR)	Chases, good to soft or softer going, not seasonal debuts
MOON OVER MIAMI (GER)	2m-2m2.5f, left-handed, recent run, preferably without headgear
MORGAN BE (GB)	Good to soft or softer going (ideally soft or heavy), preferably at Ayr
MR BIG (IRE)	Cheekpieces, preferably on good or faster going and in a big field
MY PETRA (GB)	Hurdles or small-field chases, preferably when fresh on good to soft or faster going
MYLORD COLLONGES (FR)	Chases of 2m-2m5f (preferably about 2m4f), cheekpieces
NACARAT (FR)	Flat tracks, preferably on soft going when fresh

NATIVE CORAL (IRE)	Fresh, preferably on a flat/sharp track (ideally Musselburgh or Perth) on good to soft or faster going
NEMETAN (FR)	Right-handed, second start onwards, preferably at Exeter over 2m3f+ (or over shorter trips if ground is good to soft or softer)
NENUPHAR COLLONGES (FR)	3m+, preferably on slow going, on a stiff/galloping track and in a small field if racing over fences
NEPTUNE COLLONGES (FR)	Small fields
NICTO DE BEAUCHENE (FR)	Chases of 11 or fewer runners, preferably on slow going and on tracks with easy fences
NOSTRINGSATTACHED (IRE)	2m4f+, good or faster going, cheekpieces, preferably over fences
NOTRE PERE (FR)	3m+, preferably on soft or heavy going (might also need first run of season)
OAKFIELD LEGEND (GB)	Chases of 2m6f+, fast ground
OFFICIER DE RESERVE (FR)	Small fields
OH CRICK (FR)	2m-2m1f, preferably in a big field
OISEAU DE NUIT (FR)	2m chases, not Wincanton, preferably on soft or heavy going
OLD BENNY (GB)	3m+ (ideally 3m4f+), preferably on good to soft or softer going
OLIVINO (GER)	Hurdles of about 2m, preferably on good or faster going and on left-handed tracks
OSCAR BAY (IRE)	Left-handed, second start onwards, ideally at about 2m4f on good or good to soft going

OUT THE BLACK (IRE)	Chases on good or faster going, preferably when fresh
PABLO DU CHARMIL (FR)	Small fields, especially first time out
PACCO (FR)	Handicaps, preferably at 2m-2m5f and after a relatively recent run
PAGAN STARPRINCESS (GB)	Fresh, preferably on soft or heavy going
PARSONS LEGACY (IRE)	Fresh, good or faster going
PASCO (SWI)	Flat tracks, preferably on good to soft or softer going
PEPSYROCK (FR)	Chases of about 2m, good to soft or faster going
PERCE ROCK (GB)	Grade 3 or lower level
PLANET OF SOUND (GB)	Left-handed, preferably below Class 1 level (might also prove best on good to soft or softer going)
POLITICAL PADDY (GB)	Consider all starts but especially interesting in cheekpieces on slow ground
POP (FR)	2m-2m4.5f, preferably over fences and in a small field
POSSOL (FR)	Fences, no headgear, preferably on second start onwards and on good to soft or faster going
PREISTS LEAP (IRE)	Gowran Park
PUNJABI (GB)	Hurdles, preferably on good or faster going
QUASAR D'OUDAIRIES (FR)	Second start onwards, good to soft or faster going (might prove best on easy tracks, especially right-handed ones)
RASLAN (GB)	Good to firm or faster going

RIMSKY (IRE) Fresh, preferably without headgear on an undulating track

RING BO REE (IRE) Handicaps

RING THE BOSS (IRE) Consider all starts but ideally at 2m3f+ on slow going

ROBY DE CIMBRE (FR) Small-field chases, preferably on fast going

ROLL ALONG (IRE) Seasonal debuts

RORY BOY (USA) Tracks other than Cheltenham, preferably on good or faster going and at 2m+

RUBY CROWN (GB) Right-handed hurdles, 2m-2m2.5f, preferably on undulating tracks

RUSSIAN TRIGGER (GB) No headgear, preferably over 3m4f+ on slow going

SANGFROID (GB) 2m3f+, no headgear

SEA WALL (GB) Fast ground, preferably when ridden by A P McCoy on a flat/easy track

SEYMOUR WELD (GB) Small fields, preferably on good ground and on easy tracks (especially Market Rasen)

SHERIFF HUTTON (IRE) 2m3f+ (might prove best at about 2m4f-2m6f), good or faster going

SILVERBURN (IRE) Second start onwards, tracks other than Cheltenham, preferably at about 2m4f on slow ground

SIMON (GB) 3m+, second start onwards, preferably on a flat track and slow ground

SIR HARRY ORMESHER (GB) Consider all starts, though likely to prove best in Class 2 or lower company on ground faster than heavy

SNAP TIE (IRE)	Fresh (six weeks+), preferably on fast ground at tracks other than Cheltenham
SOMETHING WELLS (FR)	Ground slower than good, trips below 3m (ideally at about 2m4f), preferably left-handed
SOUTH O'THE BORDER (GB)	Right-handed, preferably on good to soft or faster going (might also prove best at 2m-2m5f)
SPANISH CRUISE (IRE)	Fast ground (might also prove best left-handed)
STAN (NZ)	Big-field chases of 2m-2m5.5f, good to soft or faster going, no headgear
STRAWBERRY (IRE)	Good to soft or softer going, ideally from 1 February until the end of the season
SUPREME DUKE (IRE)	Right-handed, fast ground, preferably in small fields
TARANIS (FR)	Fresh
TARTAK (FR)	Flat tracks, preferably at 2m-2m5f
TATENEN (FR)	Fresh, ideally at about 2m on slow ground
THE REAL DEAL (IRE)	Good to soft or softer going, fresh, preferably in handicaps over 3m+
THE SAWYER (BEL)	Soft or heavy going, preferably at 2m3f-2m5f during January
THE VERY MAN (IRE)	Soft or heavy going, preferably at 2m7f+ on a sharp track (might also prefer a small field)
THEATRE DIVA (IRE)	Right-handed, 2m-2m5.5f, preferably in a small field during December/January
THEATRICAL MOMENT (USA)	3m+, preferably right-handed on good to soft or faster going
TIME FOR RUPERT (IRE)	2m3f+, preferably on a sharp/easy track

TOT O'WHISKEY (GB)   Fresh (first three runs), preferably on slow going, on a stiff track and in Class 3 or lower company

TRAMANTANO (GB)   Fresh, preferably on seasonal debut and on good to soft or softer going

TRICKY TRICKSTER (IRE)   Chases of 3m+, preferably on slow ground

TURKO (FR)   Grade 2 or lower, preferably in small fields, on slow ground and away from Cheltenham

VICTORY GUNNER (IRE)   Small-field chases (11 or less), preferably from late December until mid-February

WISE MEN SAY (IRE)   2m-2m2.5f, good to soft or softer going